TrixBox Made Easy

A step-by-step guide to installing and running your
home and office VoIP system

Barrie Dempster

Kerry Garrison

[PACKT] PUBLISHING

BIRMINGHAM - MUMBAI

TrixBox Made Easy

First published: September 2006

Production Reference: 2220906

Published by Packt Publishing Ltd.
32 Lincoln Road
Olton
Birmingham, B27 6PA, UK.

ISBN 1-904811-93-0

www.packtpub.com

Cover Image by www.visionwt.com

Credits

Authors

Barrie Dempster

Kerry Garrison

Reviewers

Johan Wijngaard

Levon Bragg

Development Editor

Louay Fatoohi

Technical Editor

Priyanka Baruah

Editorial Manager

Dipali Chittar

Indexer

Mithil Kulkarni

Proofreader

Chris Smith

Layouts and Illustrations

Shantanu Zagade

Cover Designer

Shantanu Zagade

About the Authors

Barrie Dempster is currently employed as a Senior Security Consultant for NGS Software Ltd., a world-renowned security consultancy well known for its focus on enterprise-level application vulnerability research and database security.

He has a background in Infrastructure and Information Security in a number of specialized environments such as financial services institutions, telecommunication companies, call centers, and other organizations across multiple continents.

Barrie has experience in the integration of network infrastructure and telecommunications systems requiring high caliber secure design, testing, and management. He has been involved in a variety of projects from the design and implementation of internet banking systems to large-scale conferencing and telephony infrastructure, as well as penetration testing and other security assessments of business-critical infrastructure.

Kerry Garrison has been in the IT industry for over 20 years with positions ranging from IT Director of a large multi-site distribution company to developing a large hosted web server platform for a major ISP, to finally running his own IT consulting business in Southern California.

Kerry was introduced to the world of Asterisk by a friend and began running his own business on it. After about a year of working with it and writing some articles that became extremely popular on the net, he felt it was time to start putting clients onto Asterisk-based systems. Today, Asterisk PBX systems represent a significant portion of his business revenue.

Kerry has spoken at Astricon and does a regular seminar series in California. He is also the publisher of both http://voipspeak.net and http://asterisktutorials.com. He is very active with the Asterisk and FreePBX community and has even contributed modules to the FreePBX project.

About the Reviewers

Johan Wijngaard has about 25 years of experience in the world of computers. He has worked with several large companies for managing middle and large networks. For the last six years, he has been active in the comunications world of Internet, PBX and Satellite, where the use of open-source has taken a big role along with Asterisk and its quick-installing brother TrixBox.

Levon Bragg is a local computer guru and co-founder of Shift Computer Services, a turn-key IT solution and service provider in Southern California. Born in 1976 in Akron, OH, Levon wrote his first computer program at the age of 9 and has been continuously expanding his knowledge and expertise across the entire landscape of Information Technology. He graduated with top honors and a degree in Computer Networking Systems Technology at ITT Technical Institute, and has several manufacturer-provided and industry certifications including 3Com's VoIP (NBX). His key field-experience highlights include implementing and supporting Microsoft's Small Business Server, Linux Servers, 3Com's NBX, and Trixbox/Asterisk.

Levon's hobbies and interests include working on and riding Harleys, photography/videography, sky-diving, video gaming, music, and working with the latest/coolest gadget/software.

Levon and his wife Jackie currently reside in Orange County, CA with Thomas their cat.

Table of Contents

Preface   1

Chapter 1: Introduction to VoIP   5
  The PSTN   5
  What is a PBX?   6
    The Traditional PBX System   7
    Hybrid PBX System   8
  VoIP   9
    Why Choose VoIP?   10
  Summary   11

Chapter 2: Introducing Asterisk   13
  Open-Source Software   13
    Facets of Open-Source Software   14
  Asterisk: The Core of TrixBox   14
    What Asterisk Isn't   15
    History of Asterisk   16
  Asterisk Features   17
  Related Websites   18
  Summary   19

Chapter 3: Introducing TrixBox   21
  Asterisk@Home to TrixBox: The Name Change   21
  TrixBox Components   21
  Difference Between Asterisk and TrixBox   22
  Prerequisite Skills   23
  The Limitations of TrixBox   23
  The Advantages of TrixBox   23
    TrixBox is Simple to Install   24
    TrixBox is Easy to Use   24

Hardware We will Need to Have   24
   Add-In Cards   25
The Future of TrixBox   26
Summary   26

Chapter 4: Planning TrixBox Deployment   27
   The Plan   27
     Extensions   28
      Number of Employees   28
      Departmental Considerations   29
     Ring Groups   31
     Call Queues   32
      Agents   33
     Connectivity   33
      PSTN   33
      VoIP   34
      ITSPs   35
      DID Lines (Direct Inward Dial)   36
     Telephones   37
      Hard Phones   37
      Soft Phones   38
     IVR (Interactive Voice Response)   39
     Fax Requirements   42
   Case Studies   42
     American Widgets Consulting Services   42
     International Widgets Call Centers Ltd   43
   Summary   44

Chapter 5: Installing TrixBox   45
   Obtain the Software   45
   Installation   45
     Media Check   47
     Automated Installation   48
   Basic System Configuration   52
     Updating TrixBox   52
     SMTP Server Setup   52
     The Web Interface   54
      Voicemail and Recordings (ARI)   55
      SugarCRM   55
      Flash Operator Panel   56
      Web MeetMe Control   57
      System Administration   58
      System Tools   62
   Summary   67

Chapter 6: TrixBox Configuration   69

FreePBX   69

Extensions   73
  Configuring our First Device   75
Trunks   79
  Setting Up a VoIP Trunk   79
  Setting Up a PSTN Trunk   84
Inbound Routing   85
Outbound Routing   87
  Dialplan Patterns   88
Digital Receptionist   89
Ring Groups   93
Queues   94
Music On-Hold   98
General Settings   99
  Dialing Options   99
  Voicemail   99
  Company Directory   100
  Fax Settings   100
  International Settings   101
  Security Settings   101

Summary   101

Chapter 7: Standard PBX Features   103

Standard Features   103

Call Forwarding   103
Call Waiting   104
Core   104
Do-Not-Disturb   104
Info Services   105
Recordings   105
Device Control   105
Active-Call Codes   105
System-Wide Speed Dialling   106
Voicemail   106
Asterisk Recording Interface (ARI)   108
Flash Operator Panel   110
  Using the Flash Operator Panel   111
Wakeup Calls   111
Weather Report   111

Summary   112

Chapter 8: Advanced TrixBox Settings — 113

Firewall Settings	113
NAT Considerations	114
Configuring Zaptel Cards	116
Configuring T1/E1 Cards	117
Overhead Paging	118
Caller-ID Blocking	120
Making Free Directory-Assistance Calls	121
Predictive Diallers	123
Advanced Reporting Tools	124
Outlook Integration	124
DISA	125
Feature Codes	125
Follow-Me	126
Misc Destinations	126
Paging and Intercom	126
Time Conditions	126
Installing WebMin	128
The Sky is the Limit	129
Summary	130

Chapter 9: SugarCRM — 131

Initial Login	131
Administration	135
User Management	136
Summary	138

Chapter 10: Securing our TrixBox Server — 139

Changing Default Passwords	140
Flash Operator Panel	141
Changing the MySQL Password	142
Connecting on a Public IP Address	143
Updating the Operating System and Asterisk	143
Backups	143
Additional Security	145
Summary	146

Appendix A: Commonly Used VoIP Terms — 147

Index — 151

Preface

TrixBox is a telephone system based on the popular open-source Asterisk PBX (Private Branch eXchange) software. TrixBox allows an individual or organization to set up a telephone system with traditional telephone networks as well as Internet-based telephony or VoIP (Voice over Internet Protocol).

This book guides the reader in the setup of this system and how to manage the telephone system. The book begins by introducing telephony concepts before detailing how to plan a telephone system and moving on to the installation, configuration, and management of a feature-packed PBX.

This book provides examples of a well laid-out telephone system with accompanying spreadsheets to aid the reader in building stable telephony infrastructure.

What This Book Covers

Chapter 1 introduces the essential telephony and IP telephony concepts to give the reader the necessary background.

Chapter 2 gives an overview of Asterisk, the PBX software at the core of TrixBox, and gives the reader a feel of the features of a powerful VoIP telephone system.

Chapter 3 explains the relationship between Asterisk and TrixBox and introduces the enhancements and power the combination of these tools provides.

Chapter 4 walks the user through planning a telephone system with accompanying spreadsheets to fill in, in order to properly plan for the installation and configuration of the system.

Chapter 5 gives the reader details on how to install TrixBox and how the basic administration components are used.

Chapter 6 applies the previous planning to the configuration of TrixBox to provide the features the reader requires from their telephone system.

Chapter 7 covers the telephone system from the point of view of the telephone handset and how the user of the telephone system can interact with it.

Chapter 8 looks at more advanced configuration options and different types of telephone line that can be managed with TrixBox.

Chapter 9 briefly introduces the SugarCRM customer relationship management tool, integrated with TrixBox.

Chapter 10 shows the reader how to secure and backup TrixBox to ensure the reliability of their system.

Appendix A has some acronyms and terms used throughout this book, which are also common terms in Telephony. This can be used as a quick reference to the terms when reading the book or configuring the TrixBox system.

What You Need for This Book

In order to install TrixBox, you need a machine that has at least a PIII 500 MHz system with 384-MB RAM and a 10-GB hard drive. Higher specifications would be necessary for production use. The machine will need a keyboard and a monitor and the ability to boot from CD-ROM initially for setup, but these won't be necessary afterwards.

For network connectivity, you will require a network card compatible with your system such as a PCI or USB network interface card. If you want to connect phone lines to your TrixBox, you will need a PCI card compatible with your connection type. We cover various connection types and list some card vendors in the book.

In order to connect to the TrixBox machine with a software-based telephone, you will need a desktop or laptop machine running a general-purpose OS such as OSX/Linux/Windows/BSD/etc. You will also need headphones and a microphone.

Conventions

In this book, you will find a number of styles of text that distinguish between different kinds of information. Here are some examples of these styles, and an explanation of their meaning.

There are three styles for code. Code words in text are shown as follows: "Once you have logged into the system, run the `genzaptelconf` script by typing `genzaptelconf` on the command line."

A block of code will be set as follows:

```
my $custpath = "city/ny";
my $filename = "new_york.txt"
```

Any command-line input and output is written as follows:

```
[root@asterisk1 ~]# genzaptelconf
```

New terms and **important words** are introduced in a bold-type font. Words that you see on the screen, in menus or dialog boxes for example, appear in our text like this: "When we are ready, we need to go to the **System Recordings** module to record our prompts".

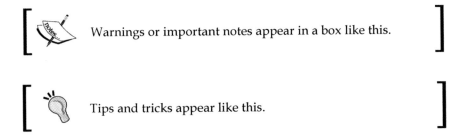

Warnings or important notes appear in a box like this.

Tips and tricks appear like this.

Reader Feedback

Feedback from our readers is always welcome. Let us know what you think about this book, what you liked or may have disliked. Reader feedback is important for us to develop titles that you really get the most out of.

To send us general feedback, simply drop an email to `feedback@packtpub.com`, making sure to mention the book title in the subject of your message.

If there is a book that you need and would like to see us publish, please send us a note in the **SUGGEST A TITLE** form on `www.packtpub.com` or email `suggest@packtpub.com`.

If there is a topic that you have expertise in and you are interested in either writing or contributing to a book, see our author guide on `www.packtpub.com/authors`.

Customer Support

Now that you are the proud owner of a Packt book, we have a number of things to help you to get the most from your purchase.

Downloading the Example Code for the Book

Visit http://www.packtpub.com/support, and select this book from the list of titles to download any example code or extra resources for this book. The files available for download will then be displayed.

The downloadable files contain instructions on how to use them.

Errata

Although we have taken every care to ensure the accuracy of our contents, mistakes do happen. If you find a mistake in one of our books—maybe a mistake in text or code—we would be grateful if you would report this to us. By doing this you can save other readers from frustration, and help to improve subsequent versions of this book. If you find any errata, report them by visiting http://www.packtpub.com/support, selecting your book, clicking on the **Submit Errata** link, and entering the details of your errata. Once your errata have been verified, your submission will be accepted and the errata added to the list of existing errata. The existing errata can be viewed by selecting your title from http://www.packtpub.com/support.

Questions

You can contact us at questions@packtpub.com if you are having a problem with some aspect of the book, and we will do our best to address it.

Introduction to VoIP

1

TrixBox is essentially an easy-to-use system for managing our telephony needs. Before we can understand how to operate the TrixBox telephone system, we need to cover the basic principles that underlie the system. In this chapter, we will talk about the telephone network and the PBX (Private Branch Exchange) that traditional telephone systems run on. Fundamentally, TrixBox is a VoIP (Voice over Internet Protocol) system. So, we will have a look at what VoIP means and why it is useful to us. We will also take a look at any prerequisite knowledge or skills required, with advice on where to get these if necessary. We will define any new terms we come across; however, some of the commonly used terms used in or relating to this book are listed in Appendix A at the end of the book for ease of reference while reading the later chapters.

The PSTN

The acronym **PSTN** stands for Public Switched Telephone Network. PSTN is the network that traditional phone systems used and was generally controlled by the telecommunication companies. This is the network our calls are travelling over when we pick up our handset and dial a number. This network spans the world and there are many different interfaces to it:

- **POTS**: POTS stands for Plain Old Telephone Service. It is commonly used for residential use. POTS is an analogue system and is controlled by electrical loops. It is provided with copper wires run to residences and places of business and is, therefore, the cheapest and easiest telephone service to roll out.

- ISDN: This is a faster and more feature-filled connection (also more expensive) This gained some popularity within small to medium-sized business as a cost-effective way of connecting to the PSTN and getting some advanced services, like many lines to one office or voice and data lines on one service. ISDN is a digital service and offers a few more features over POTS.

- T1/E1: This is more expensive and used for high-volume data and voice networks. It is more common in larger companies, although in recent years it has become more affordable. T1/E1 is also a digital service and offers yet more features than ISDN, the most important feature being increased bandwidth that translates, in telephony, to more telephone lines.

The trouble with PSTN is that it's very static and in most countries it is strictly controlled by the telecommunication companies. If a business wants to make a lot of internal calls using the PSTN, it is by no means a cheap way to communicate. ISDN/T1/E1 are most commonly found at the external interface of a company's communication network, with all the internal communications going through internal lines that are controlled by an internal telephone system.

What is a PBX?

A **PBX** is an acronym for a Private Branch eXchange, which provides for the internal telephone system. Telephone exchanges were initially under the control of the telephone providers, such as AT&T in the US or British Telecom in the UK. These companies handled all line provisioning and call routing between the businesses and the public. Initially, the routing of calls was done by a team of operators (usually female) sitting in the offices of the telephone companies and routing calls by plugging and unplugging cables to connect one caller to another. Eventually, as the reliance and the demands of this service grew, technology evolved to the point where we had automatic systems managing these calls.

As the modern telephone networks began to take shape, private companies saw a greater reliance on telephone communication. Many decided to implement their own services so that they could handle calls internal to the organization. Usually, the equipment was leased or bought from the telephone companies mentioned previously, so they were quite happy to help with these services. These companies also got to charge for the lines and calls connecting the company externally, and so they could profit from this too. As we saw in the previous section, the more expensive digital lines were now being used only as a means of communicating outside the building, rather than using externally provided lines for all communication.

At this point, it became obvious that there was a need for these companies to install their own telephone equipment to route internal calls and, in some cases, to make sure calls going out or coming into the company went via the correct routes. For example, you don't want Alice in accounting calling Bob in HR through a line that leaves the company and crosses continents if they sit within the same building. Therefore, there is a requirement for a PBX to effectively manage calls and ensure that they go via the most cost effective and reliable routes in order to keep the company communicating internally between departments and employees, and externally with customers and suppliers.

In its basic form, a PBX is the interface between the public telephone network and the private network within the company. Since most companies need fewer phones lines than the number of employees they have, they can get away by having a few outgoing lines but many internal extensions so that employees can converse internally. This costs little more than the maintenance of the PBX and internal cabling, and there are no line rentals or other call charges being paid to the telecommunications provider. The PBX then handles all of the routing in and out of the company using the lines effectively. The PBX also handles calls within the company so that a call from one internal phone to another does not have to go out onto the phone circuits and back in.

As PBXs became more common, businesses and their employees required more features and functionality such as voicemail, call parking, call transfers, music on-hold, IVR menus, least-cost routing, and an Automatic Call Distributor (ACD) in order to provide for calling groups. With the increase in demand for communications in all aspects of a business, the features required in a phone system become more complex and more expensive. If modern companies had to rely on the telecommunications provider for all these features, the cost of communication could become prohibitively high.

The Traditional PBX System

It is not hard to spot a traditional PBX system. It is usually a large box full of mechanical switches and relays mounted on a wall in 'the phone room'. When a company's requirement changes, they generally contact their PBX provider who will charge varying rates to make hardware and configuration changes to fit the new requirements. With PBXs being very complicated and each differing from the others greatly, it can take a considerable level of training and experience to provide the support for a busy PBX system. This leads to most PBX customers relying on their PBX suppliers for, often expensive, support. So while by bringing the communications internally businesses could benefit from savings on line rentals, they still often had a reliance on their providers for support. Often, the companies selling and supporting the PBXs were the same telecommunication companies providing the external lines.

With a traditional PBX system we would also almost always purchase our phone system from the same manufacturer as the PBX system, usually with very few options to choose from when it comes to contract options and hardware such as telephone handsets or headsets. Adding features like voicemail can usually be an expensive add-on to the base system, sometimes requiring an entirely new piece of equipment! A traditional PBX system has the following structure:

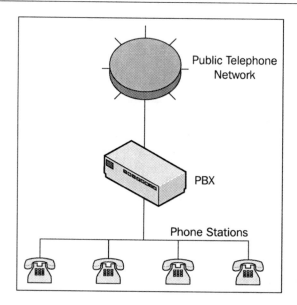

Although some legacy PBX systems now have options for network access and VoIP functionality, these options are often very expensive upgrades and they generally lack the features and configuration options in the newer VoIP systems.

Hybrid PBX System

A hybrid PBX system combines the features of a traditional PBX system with VoIP functionality. In some cases, the VoIP functionality may just be the way the PBX communicates with the phones. Some other VoIP functionalities may include the ability to have remote extensions or **Soft Phones**, and the ability to use Internet Telephone Service Providers (ITSPs) and not just the traditional public telephone network. The main added benefit is the combined functionality, as we can keep all our existing lines and numbers and add in VoIP for substantial savings where possible.

The Asterisk PBX system is a full hybrid system combining numerous types of connections to the public telephone network as well as VoIP functionality including:

- Use of industry-standard SIP-compliant phones
- Remote extensions using either SIP-compliant phones, or Soft Phones
- Support for IAX (Inter-Asterisk eXchange)
- Bridging remote Asterisk systems together to act as a single system

Following is an example of a hybrid PBX system:

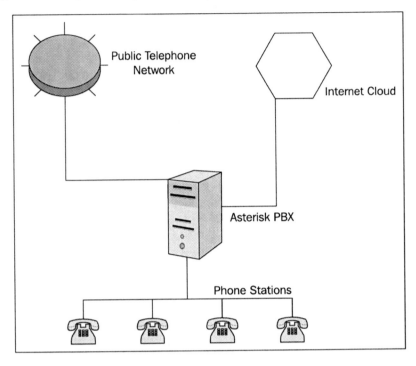

VoIP

We have covered, in brief, how a traditional PBX system could lack some of the features of a Voice over Internet Protocol system and discovered some of the basics of the PSTN. We can now take a look at VoIP in a little bit more detail to get an idea of what the benefits are.

Firstly, it's important to realize that VoIP doesn't entirely replace the PSTN (although it could). VoIP is yet another, cheaper, and easier way to connect to the PSTN. You can make and receive calls that are initiated and terminated entirely across VoIP and you can call a standard PSTN number from VoIP and vice-versa, as long as your ITSP (Internet Telephony Service Provider) supports it or if you link your VoIP system to the PSTN yourself. Both of these are options to consider with TrixBox.

A VoIP system can use a variety of protocols and we will cover each of those protocols relevant to TrixBox as we come across them. VoIP is a catch-all term for these protocols and refers to transferring voice data over the Internet.

As the Internet grew and became a more flexible system than the PSTN, it became apparent that it was possible and, in many cases, preferable to use the Internet for carrying voice as well as data. There were a few limitations that had to be overcome before this could be feasible. For example, data connections can tolerate some latency in communication but latency in voice can be very annoying as it leads to gaps in conversation and constant repetition. Watching a news broadcast from a reporter using a satellite phone is a very good example of how frustrating and error prone this form of communication can be. As Internet connection latency decreased and speeds increased, voice communication has become more viable.

There is a tendency to think of VoIP as a new technology. However, it is almost two decades old and has only recently become so popular because there are now a few good pieces of software that use this technology. There are also many companies investing in VoIP, since the data lines that provide Internet services are now at a level where they are usually reliable enough to be used for voice communication. Customers and employees expect these data lines to be low-latency, clear, and always available. While many Internet services still have problems, the situation is certainly much better than it was in the late 80s and early 90s when VoIP was first touted as the killer technology. It wasn't quite there then, but is certainly getting there now.

Why Choose VoIP?

The most important facet of VoIP is that it is "over Internet Protocol". This means that it benefits from the layered design of Internet communication and can be a very flexible communication mechanism. A VoIP implementation can generally be shifted from one service provider to another with little or no effect on the systems in use. Anyone that has gone through the nightmare of moving just a single telephone number between providers will realize the benefit VoIP brings in this area. Flexibility in communication is an important aspect for businesses as it helps to control the business process.

VoIP is also many times cheaper than traditional telephone services as it can be routed over a variety of cheap lines. The most important aspect here is usually the long distance rates. Calls can traverse the Internet until they get to the same country, state, or city as the recipient before touching the PSTN and in some cases bypass the PSTN entirely, meaning that we are no longer shackled to our telecommunications provider. We can pick and choose from the many Internet Providers and/or Internet Telephone Service Providers. The one downside to VoIP is that Internet connections are often less stable than the PSTN and therefore we can have occasional downtime in our telephony service. This can be mitigated by having multiple providers with failover, something which is near to impossible or prohibitively expensive with a PSTN service!

Before choosing VoIP, we should carefully examine the available service plans and options of the available PSTN providers as well as the ISP/ITSPs in our area. It's important to determine our current costs, our current needs, and the features we require in our telephone system as well as what we expect these needs to grow to in the foreseeable future. Armed with this information, we can make a valid choice as to which communication medium is the most appropriate and cost effective for our business.

Summary

In this chapter, we have covered the basic background to the traditional telephone network and have introduced VoIP as a cost-saving and flexible system for managing our telephone system. We've introduced some of the terminology we will be using throughout the book. There is, however, a more detailed list in Appendix A. We should have an understanding of why VoIP is growing in popularity and why it may be a sensible choice for our needs. The chapter also provided us with a good understanding of what a PBX is and what makes a VoIP PBX different from a traditional PBX system.

2
Introducing Asterisk

In this chapter, we will be looking at what Asterisk is, and what it can do for us. As we explore the features, we can make note of what will help us to accomplish our goals and be useful in our environment. Creating a phone system based on Asterisk is an affordable alternative to a traditional PBX system. As we plan our deployment we will need to have an idea of the features we will use.

Open-Source Software

The concept behind open-source software is that not only is the application available to the general public at no cost, but the actual source code that created the application is also available and freely distributable. This allows other users of the application to make changes to the source code and optionally pass these changes on to other users of the software.

Asterisk and the other components of TrixBox, however, are released under the GPL (General Public License) that comes with the caveat that when someone makes changes to the original code and decides to distribute the modified version they have to provide it under the same license. There is no obligation to distribute the source code, but if we choose to we must release it under the GPL.

GPL

The GPL is a license produced by GNU (http://www.gnu.org) and is one of the most common licenses used by open-source software. There are many other open-source licenses recognized by the OSI (Open-Source Initiative) (http://www.opensource.org).

Facets of Open-Source Software

The main advantage of using open-source software is that the software is free. Some open-source software can even rival the quality of some commercial packages. Some good examples of top-notch open-source software include Open Office (`http://www.openoffice.org`), GIMP (`http://www.gimp.org`), and Gaim (`http://gaim.sourceforge.net`).

There are thousands of open-source projects to choose from. The largest repository can be found at `http://www.sourceforge.net`.

Of course, something as good as open-source software cannot come without a catch. Since all the programming and development is done by individuals, there are often no companies to complain to when something doesn't work right. For the more popular open-source projects, some companies have sprung up to provide support. When making a decision to use open-source software, we should make sure that our own staff can provide the support for the application or that we have a reliable source of support, should the need arise. However, some projects have a large amount of input and support from a sponsor company, as is the case with Digium and Asterisk, and these companies know the product inside out and can provide a very high level of support for the project. There are also many support companies and consultants that will offer services in relation to Asterisk.

Since there are a number of different open-source licensing models, we must understand the ramifications of using a particular piece of open-source code. If we are developing a particular application and decide to use some open-source code from certain licenses and plan to distribute our changes as a product, we may be required to contribute our entire improved code back to community as open-source code as well

Asterisk: The Core of TrixBox

Asterisk is basically a telephony toolkit enabling developers to create numerous types of applications that interface with telephone networks. The most obvious application is that of a PBX. Asterisk can also be used as an IVR (Interactive Voice Response) system, for teleconferences and as a voicemail system. These functions can also be combined to create a powerful multi-faceted telecommunication system, which is the focus of this book. Asterisk is, however, most commonly used to build hybrid PBX systems that utilize modern PCI cards instead of banks of switches and relays, and software instead of custom hardware. By using relatively simple PCI cards in a standard x86 computer system running on Linux, the cost to build a working system is greatly reduced as compared to the often expensive and inflexible traditional PBX.

Asterisk PBX is, simply put, just software. While different hardware connectivity components are available, all of the features and routing is done through software. This is an amazing technical breakthrough considering that even the most modern PBX systems still rely completely on proprietary hardware and electronic switches and relays, and require specialized technicians to install and maintain. The costs for a telephone engineer to work on these systems can be extremely expensive.

By implementing the functionality completely through software, this opens up countless possibilities for even more advanced features such as predictive diallers, database integration, and virtually anything we could imagine doing with a phone system. All this and much more can be accomplished with a little ingenuity and a little programming. We don't have to be a programmer to run an Asterisk system unless we want to extend its functionality. Although some people, who are looking for very specific functions to be created, will post bounties that programmers can collect on by writing pieces of code, these bounties are another function of open-source software that isn't generally available in a closed-source model. This is a good way to get functionality required within your system and is also a good way of giving back to the project as it supports programmers and the ongoing development of Asterisk. However, this isn't a necessity as Asterisk has an extremely strong following and many large companies now rely on Asterisk for their telephony and in some cases for their revenue as they sell products and services based on Asterisk. For example, there are many ITSPs that use Asterisk to manage their infrastructure and sell VoIP services to businesses and the general public the world over.

With so many organizations relying on Asterisk for their businesses, the most common and some of the not-so-common functions that could be required of a PBX system have generally been developed and tested widely in quite demanding environments.

What Asterisk Isn't

Asterisk by itself is not an easy system to set up and maintain. There are dozens of configuration files that need to be edited and maintained. There is no included interface to set up and configure Asterisk. Moreover, the few available management tools have to be installed and configured separately. However, the benefit of TrixBox is that much of this is hidden away from the user and with the aid of this book it should be much easier to get a functional and useful system up and running. Asterisk on its own is not:

- A plug-and-play telephone system or IVR system
- Easy to configure without training and/or adequate documentation
- A full hardware solution
- The complete solution to every business's communication needs
- Useful without telephony expertise

While Digium does offer a Business Edition of Asterisk, the open-source version does not come with any technical support. Being an open-source project, we either need to be able to troubleshoot it ourselves, turn to community forums for support, or hire a consultant to help us out.

If we are already fairly proficient with Linux, we are well ahead of the crowd that typically looks at the TrixBox system. While Asterisk is just another software package that runs on almost every Linux distribution, TrixBox is a distribution of its own, which abstracts some of these, sometimes complicated, layers from us. So at some point, Linux skills may be helpful for optimal system tuning but are by no means a necessity. As we will see shortly, when we look closer at TrixBox, TrixBox can make many of these issues much less of a concern and more straightforward.

You can't install Asterisk on your standard PC and then plug into any PSTN interface you choose without the correct hardware. If we want to access the PSTN (which is by no means a requirement), we may want to get services from an ITSP or install hardware in our server in order to provide access to our POTS, ISDN, and other line types.

History of Asterisk

Asterisk was originally created by Mark Spencer, the CEO and founder of Digium Ltd. While Asterisk is a fully open-source product, Digium manufactures hardware components for connecting to the public telephone network. Digium has a complete range of cards from analog cards, with the ability to support 1 to 24 analog lines, to digital interface cards to connect to T1/E1 lines that can support from 1 to 4 circuits. There are also other cards available from other suppliers and you can use standard modems such as those used in dial-up Internet access. The Digium hardware is the best tested and documented when it comes to use with Asterisk though.

The Business Edition of Asterisk offered by Digium is more fully tested, documented, and also includes technical support. This allows businesses that are uncomfortable with a fully open-source solution to purchase more of a boxed-copy version. While the Business Edition has to go through a long certification test process by Digium, the open-source version is tested by beta testers in the Asterisk community.

What started off simply as a side project changed almost overnight when Mark Spencer hooked up with Jim Dixon who was working on the Zapata drivers. All of a sudden Asterisk had a means of connecting to the telephone network. The telephony revolution had begun.

On September 23, 2004, Mark Spencer released the 1.0.0 version of Asterisk during his keynote speech at the first **AstriCon**, which is the official Asterisk user and developer's conference. Just over a year later, the stable version 1.0.9 was released and is now quite locked down as far as its features go.

Asterisk Features

Amazingly enough, Asterisk has more features than most traditional PBX systems, which are composed of a large box full of hardware. Hence, the Asterisk mantra of 'it's just software'. The following is only a partial list of the many features included with Asterisk:

- **Automated Attendant**: An automated system for answering incoming calls and routing them based on the caller's responses to voice prompts.

- **Blacklists**: Blacklisting is the ability to easily add numbers to a central database that will prevent calls from the blacklisted phone numbers being processed by the system.

- **Call Detail Records**: The detailed call reports and usage statistics to show an administrator the activity of the phone system.

- **Call Forward on Busy**: This feature automatically forwards a call to another extension if the called extension is busy.

- **Call Forward on No Answer**: This feature automatically forwards a call to another extension if the called extension does not answer.

- **Call Parking**: This feature refers to placing a call into a holding state so that it can be picked up at another extension.

- **Call Queuing**: A system that allows inbound callers to sit in a holding room listening to music on-hold until the next available agent is available to speak to them.

- **Call Recording**: The ability to record inbound or outbound calls to .wav files.

- **Call Routing**: Based on the phone number that was dialed (DID) or the number that was called from (ANI), a call can be routed to a specified extension, group, queue, etc.

- **Call Transfer**: This refers to the ability to transfer an existing call to another extension.

- **Caller-ID**: Caller-ID is used to display the phone number and other available information of the user that is calling into the system.

- **Conference Bridging**: Asterisk has the ability to create conference rooms that multiple people can attend at one time for group meetings.

- **Interactive Directory Listing**: A Company directory system that can look up users by first or last name.

- **Interactive Voice Response (IVR)**: This system uses pre-recorded voice menus to prompt callers to make selections via their phone such as *"press 1 for sales, 2 for support"*.

- **Music On-Hold**: Asterisk can play MP3 files to callers who are on-hold or waiting in a queue.

- **Remote Office Support**: Asterisk uses Internet Protocols for communication. Hence, users can be at remote locations and have access to the system via broadband Internet connection.

- **VoIP Gateways**: Using the new Internet Telephone Service Providers (ITSPs), an Asterisk system can have telephone network connectivity without having to use a normal analog service provider.

- **Voicemail**: Each user in an Asterisk system can have their extension and voicemail account. Using TrixBox, the voicemail can be retrieved via their phone, from a remote location, sent via email, or accessed via a web browser.

At the time of writing, Asterisk was at version 1.2 branch. Some of the new features in this version include:

- A new dynamic IVR (Interactive Voice Response) flow-control interface
- PRI improvement
- SIP support improvements
- Customized CDR (Call Detail Record) support
- A real-time database configuration storage engine
- A new real-time interface that allows for faster and less disruptive configuration changes
- New dial plan syntax and a new dial plan language, including many new applications and dial plan functions
- Improvements in protocol handling for better voice quality

Related Websites

There are a number of good information sites for additional Asterisk information. A few of the more popular ones are:

- `http://www.trixbox.org`: This is the official TrixBox website.
- `http://www.asterisk.org`: This is the official Asterisk website.
- `http://forums.digium.com`: This is Digium's support forums website.
- `http://voip-info.org/wiki`: The most complete wiki site for all VoIP-related queries.
- `http://VOIPSpeak.net`: Kerry Garrison's site containing articles, news, and tutorials on numerous VoIP topics.

- `http://www.asteriskdocs.org`: This is the home of the Asterisk User Documentation Project.

For further information, you can also refer to the book *Building Telephony Systems with Asterisk* from Packt Publishing (ISBN 1-904811-15-9) also co-authored by Barrie Dempster.

Summary

In this chapter, we have introduced Asterisk as an open-source PBX with just a glimpse of the hundreds of features that are built into the system. There are many other features, and since Asterisk has a built-in programming language, many new features can be, and have been, added by end users and programmers. We will see some of these customizations in the later chapters. We also have an idea of the history of Asterisk and why it came into fairly popular use. We have information on websites and books for further information on Asterisk, if necessary. However, from now onwards we will be very TrixBox specific with our discussion.

3
Introducing TrixBox

TrixBox was created by Andrew Gillis in November, 2004 with the goal of enabling a home user to build a fully functional Asterisk PBX system without needing to be a Linux guru or knowing much about telephony; however, it has grown beyond that significantly. TrixBox consists of a downloadable ISO. By booting a computer off the CD image, the system will format our hard drive, install TrixBox along with CentOs and a number of associated tools and utilities. By packaging a complete operating system and a scripted install of all the applications, we are assured of being able to get a basic system up and running with very little effort or knowledge involved.

Asterisk@Home to TrixBox: The Name Change

TrixBox was originally called Asterisk@Home. However, the name was recently changed for a number of reasons. There are two main reasons, namely, Asterisk is a trademark of Digium Ltd, and the "@Home" portion of the name may serve to downplay the usefulness and features of TrixBox, which is quite capable of providing the traditional telephone needs and VoIP needs of small and medium businesses.

TrixBox Components

The TrixBox system is made up of a number of components each of which is released under an open-source license. The main benefit of TrixBox is that these components are preinstalled and configured to run. This reduces the effort involved in setting up these applications as compared to trying to accomplish this manually. At the time of writing, TrixBox was at version 1.0 and contained the following components:

- **CentOS 4.3**: CentOS is a community supported version of the Red Hat Enterprise Linux distribution as well as the Linux distribution that TrixBox is based on.

- **Asterisk 1.2**: The core of the entire system is the most recent version of Asterisk open-source PBX.

- **FreePBX**: This tool provides a web-based interface to manage and maintain our Asterisk installation.

- **Flash Operator Panel (FOP)**: The Flash Operator Panel is a switchboard application that a receptionist can use to see the status of all the extensions and telephone circuits.

- **Cisco XML Services**: If we are using Cisco IP phones, this tool will help create all the configuration files needed to provision for these phones.

- **SugarCRM**: SugarCRM is a Customer Relationship Management system for tracking sales leads, customer contacts, etc. It has nice integration with Asterisk and has recently inked a deal with Microsoft that will allow SugarCRM to be released under the Microsoft Community License.

- **Automated Installation Tools**: All the tools, operating system, scripts, and config files are automatically installed and configured for use by the TrixBox setup script.

- **Festival Speech Engine**: Many of the functions within Asterisk require some text-to-speech capability. The Festival speech engine provides that functionality.

- **Weather AGI script**: The Weather script is a great example of things that can be accomplished with Asterisk. This script can be modified to pull down a text file from a weather service and read it back to a caller using the Festival text-to-speech engine.

- **Wakeup AGI script**: This is another good scripting example. This script asks the caller for a time at which he/she would like to get a reminder call. At the specified time, the user's extension is dialed and a reminder tone is played.

- **Digium Card auto-config**: For systems that will be using Digium hardware, an automatic configuration script takes care of the initial configuration of the required configuration files.

Difference Between Asterisk and TrixBox

The simplest way of looking at it is that Asterisk is simply one of the many components of TrixBox. While Asterisk is the actual PBX software, TrixBox is a self-installing package that installs a complete operating system, Asterisk PBX, and all the supporting components as listed in the previous section.

The core strength of TrixBox lies in its simple setup and FreePBX (the web interface). This book will cover FreePBX in detail for the configuration of our PBX system as well as the other components.

To get an Asterisk system up and running, we would have to pick a supported Linux distribution, install the distribution, configure it securely, and then install Asterisk and configure that. With TrixBox we have one installation routine, which not only gives us a fully functioning operating system with Asterisk installed but also pre-installs all the other components for us.

Prerequisite Skills

The basic setup and configuration of TrixBox is fairly easy. However, to properly maintain and troubleshoot the system we may need a basic level of Linux skills such as how to update the operating system, how to navigate through the command-line interface, and how to download, compile, and install different software packages. We won't cover basic Linux skills in details here, but we will walkthrough many of the important areas when they relate to performing functions relating to TrixBox.

The Limitations of TrixBox

Die-hard Asterisk purists will insist that by using TrixBox we are seriously crippling the abilities of the system. The reality is that we can do almost anything with a TrixBox installation just as we can with a bare Asterisk installation. The main limitation we have is that FreePBX requires a specific layout of configuration files, and any hand editing could be overwritten or could break the FreePBX interface.

TrixBox also locks us down to one machine. When it comes to having multiple machines handling our telephony, it can be difficult to migrate from TrixBox to multiple Asterisk boxes as the TrixBox interface only allows for single machine architecture. This can be manageable as long as the administrators configuring the telephone system are aware of the need to log in to multiple interfaces in order to make changes. As the telephony infrastructure and required capacity grows, it can become quite difficult to manage. It's worth considering moving directly to multiple Asterisk systems rather than trying to run concurrent TrixBox systems.

Basically, as our needs grow towards those of a large business TrixBox becomes less useful to us. However, for small and medium businesses it can perform well and meet most needs, from small shops to busy call centres.

The Advantages of TrixBox

TrixBox comes with a number of custom applications that have been created specifically for TrixBox. These applications show just how powerful and flexible the TrixBox system really is. Much of this code was created by the **Advanced TrixBox Users Group** and has been donated back to the community for anyone to use.

TrixBox is Simple to Install

TrixBox is very easy to set up and manage. In just a few minutes, we can have the system fully installed and we can spend the majority of the time performing the important tasks relating to configuring our phone system. The TrixBox website is located at http://www.trixbox.org/. Once we download the ISO image, we will need to burn it to a CD with our favorite CD-burning software. Having done so, the TrixBox package couldn't be easier to install. As we boot off the CD that we made from the ISO image, we will be presented with the CentOS installation screen. All we have to do is hit the *ENTER* key, and we will be prompted for our location and a password for the root user. The rest of the installation is completely automatic.

Typically, we need to be well versed in Linux with a general knowledge of telephony in order to set up and configure an Asterisk PBX system. However, with TrixBox, virtually anyone can get a system up and running. All we need to know to follow along with this book is how to burn an image to a CD and how to boot our computer using a CD. Everything else we need to know will be taught step by step throughout this book. Since the installation is simply a one-key installation, there is no special Linux voodoo needed to get everything up and running.

TrixBox is Easy to Use

Once the system is operational, only very basic commands are needed to do some system maintenance and to monitor the system for troubleshooting purposes. Unless we are building a system for a large number of users, trying to bridge multiple systems together, or add software hard-disk mirroring, this book will show us everything we need to install and configure our system. However, for long-term maintenance and troubleshooting, a basic level of Linux skills will come in handy.

For advanced configurations and setting up different hardware components, Linux administration knowledge will prove to be very useful, especially when it comes to troubleshooting configuration files, getting devices to function properly, and setting up automated tasks.

Hardware We will Need to Have

The TrixBox package will install on pretty minimal hardware. For prototyping and experimenting, we can use a system as low as a PIII 500 MHz system with 384-MB RAM and a 10-GB hard drive. The system will need to be able to boot from a CD-ROM drive. A keyboard and a monitor are only required during the initial setup. If we are planning on putting the system to use in a business environment, these minimum requirements are not going to be sufficient. A business class machine should consist of at least a 2.0 GHz processor with 1 GB RAM and a 100 GB hard disk. Some users have reported good results with lesser systems but we run the risk of poor playback and recording of sound files that can dramatically reduce the quality of the user experience. We also have to ensure that we keep adequate disk space available as this could severely impact the performance of the system.

It is highly recommended that even if we are not planning on connecting our system to any traditional phone circuits, we should get at least one FXO card to provide Asterisk with a good timing signal to prevent problems with voicemail and audio prompts. There are numerous online retailers providing compatible cards. A good starter kit would be the **Digium Developer's Kit** which includes a card, one FXO module, and one FXS module. This provides us with the scope for adding one telephone line and one traditional telephone. If we have a requirement for more lines or telephones, then we should ensure that we buy cards with enough ports.

Numerous problems occur when Asterisk does not have a good timing signal or when the server itself is not adequate. One of the biggest sources of problems arises from using a cheap motherboard. Many of the budget motherboards, most notably ones with one, two, or three PCI slots, use a shared IRQ system, which can cause compatibility issues with add-in cards and will result in poor performance and greatly reduced sound quality. A system like this may be fine for our house and when just testing things out, but we will want a good quality system for running a business on. When choosing our hardware components, refer to the current documentation in the Asterisk and TrixBox wiki pages. There is a list available on Digium's website that lists currently recommended motherboards.

Timing problems really become tricky when the system has to convert from one audio format to another. For example, if our phones are communicating with our Asterisk server using the **iLBC codec** and our system is communicating with an Internet Telephone Service Provider (ITSP) using the **g711u codec**, then the Asterisk server has to convert the audio from iLBC to g711u format. If our system does not have a good timing signal, then the end result will be very poor sound quality. If we are using a Digium card or compatible hardware, then the card will provide the timing signal that Asterisk needs in order to function properly.

We can think of a timing signal as a system-generated heartbeat that allows different processes to stay in sync. With Asterisk 1.2, the kernel provides its own timing signal, which does away with the need for a hardware replacement signal.

Add-In Cards

For experimenting or for very small systems, we can get very inexpensive cards to connect our system to POTS (Plain Old Telephone Service) lines. These cheap FXO cards, often referred to as **X100P** cards, can be found on eBay for about $10.00. The

X100P card is basically an Intel WinModem with a specific chipset that is capable of working with Asterisk. This card is used to connect a single analog phone line to an Asterisk server. However, if we are going to use only Internet Telephone Service Providers, then we will not need any additional hardware.

Digium manufactures a complete line of expansion cards to fill PSTN (Public Switched Telephone Network) connectivity ranging from multi-port POTS connections to cards supporting up to four T1 lines (equivalent to 96 individual phone lines).

The full range of Digium products can be found in the **Products** section of its website at `http://www.digium.com/en/products/`. Other suppliers of compatible cards include:

- Rhino Equipment at `http://www.rhinoequipment.com/`
- Sangoma at `http://www.sangoma.com/`
- VoIPSupply at `http://www.voipsupply.com`

The Future of TrixBox

The TrixBox version 1.0 contains Asterisk 1.2, the latest version of FreePBX, and the Flash Operator Panel. This is a powerful combination of tools, which will enable some incredible functionality that other systems can only dream of having. In the near future, TrixBox will contain automated telephone-provisioning tools, additional third-party software, and a simplified updating mechanism.

TrixBox version 1.1 was released as this book neared completion and contains the latest versions of the tools included with TrixBox 1.0 and also adds in **Munin** (`http://munin.projects.linpro.no/`), which is an open-source package for monitoring and maintaining your operating system.

Summary

We should now have a good understanding of what the TrixBox system is and how it is different from Asterisk by itself. We should also have a good idea by now if this is the direction we want to go with building our PBX system. In the following chapters, we go into the design, installation, and configuration of our system.

4
Planning TrixBox Deployment

When planning for a production PBX system, we hope to spend more time in the planning stage than in actually building the system. A poorly designed system will make for numerous changes after the system is up and running. Most businesses will not tolerate too many changes after their telephone system is supposed to be fully functional. Proper planning also reduces the administrative burden. We should ensure that we plan adequately in order to create a system that fits the needs of our business, since reconfiguration of a live system can often lead to downtime.

To help plan and deploy our system, we will go through each of the primary functions and see what role these functions play in a deployment plan. We will look at some planning spreadsheets as examples so that we can apply these when planning our systems. We will achieve this through a couple of case studies that will give us a realistic view of the planning process as far as possible.

The spreadsheets that accompany this chapter can be downloaded from the book's website at http://www.packtpub.com/support.

The Plan

There are a number of areas we need to consider when building our telephone system, such as the physical infrastructure for the stability and security of the system, the need to lock the PBX, the need to provide adequate heating control, and so on. Most of this is very specific to our environment and is covered well in the documentation on infrastructure and maintaining service-level agreements (SLAs). Besides these, the most important areas, on which this chapter focuses, are those relating to the configuration of the PBX system itself. We will need to consider the following:

- Extensions
- Ring groups
- Call queues

- Connectivity
    - ° PSTN
    - ° VoIP
    - ° ITSPs
    - ° DID Lines (Direct Inward Dial)
- Telephones
    - ° Hard phones
    - ° Soft phones
- IVR (Interactive Voice Response)
- Fax requirements

These are the main, or most common, areas of concern when planning our deployment. We will cover each of these in detail and then look at case studies implementing these.

Extensions

If we ask ten telephone engineers about the probable length of our extensions, we will get ten different answers. Some will say to use the shortest length possible to support our actual extensions, others have lookup charts to help figure it out, and still others use some unknown mysticism to conjure up the optimal extension length.

Of course, there are simple methods and a few key points that we have to take into consideration.

Number of Employees

Even in an office of less than ten people, we should never recommend using single-digit extensions. This is extremely limiting not only from a headcount perspective, but also very limiting in terms of voice menus that may play to our advantage. In the mid 90's, the World Wide Web was becoming the great equalizer. Small mom-and-pop shops could put up websites and compete on the Web against huge global corporations. With an Asterisk-based PBX system, a small business with just a few employees could sound like a Fortune-500 company when its clients, vendors, or even competitors call in. Hence, for a business of any size, having an introductory announcement saying *"Thank you for calling the Acme Widget Company; press 1 for Kerry, 2 for John, or 3 for David"* does not portray much in the way of professionalism.

Even if there are only three employees in the company, a far better approach would be to have an announcement that says *"Thank you for calling the Acme Widget Company; if you know the extension of the party you are calling, you may enter it at any time; to speak directly to an agent, press the # key. For Sales press 1, for Billing press 2, for Marketing press 3; please make your selection now"*. This gives a more professional appearance to the company. If this is the first time a person is trying to contact our company, we want them to feel that they are in the hands of professionals of whatever trade or business we are in. It also gives us room for expansion and staff changes. If our company suddenly grows or an employee is replaced we wouldn't have to reconfigure the phone system to reflect this.

This approach also applies to face-to-face meetings. Consider the following two business cards. The first one gives away the fact that there are probably only a few employees in the company and may give a negative impression to clients.

Kerry Garrison
(949) 555-1212 ext. 2

Versus

Kerry Garrison
(949) 555-1212 ext. 202

We should keep in mind the actual numbering scheme. For the sake of smooth functionality, we should avoid using extensions that begin with any of the numbers we may use in our IVR menus. If we use menus like *"Press 1 for Sales, 2 for Billing, and 3 for Support"*, then we should try to avoid using extensions that begin with 1, 2, or 3. If we cannot avoid using these numbers, it will not seriously impact our system, but it can introduce unwelcome delays while the system is trying to figure out if it needs to go to a menu or an extension. It's also a good idea to group extensions where possible, so we have specific ranges for specific functions of the system.

Departmental Considerations

When planning our extensions, we need to remember that there are more areas of the telephone system, such as ring groups and queues, than the actual phones using extension numbers. From an organizational point of view, most companies will group extensions based on department such as 2xx for Sales, 3xx for Marketing, and 4xx for Support. The same works well for organizing ring groups and queues. Using the last example, we might use 200 for the Sales queue, 300 for the Marketing queue, and so on.

While using a fixed method like this may not be the most efficient number scheme in terms of using all the numbers in a range, it does allow for a large amount of growth, changes, and flexibility.

As an exercise for creating our extension list, first start by grouping our company into groups such as departments, create a list of queues if we are going to use them, and create a list of ring groups.

- Sales:
  - David: 201
  - John: 202
- Marketing:
  - Karen: 301
  - Maurice: 302
- Support:
  - Kerry: 401
- Sales Ring Group (2000): David, John
- Support Call Queue (4000): Kerry, David, Maurice

There are no rules that say how we should pick extension numbers for users, ring groups, or queues. However, from a maintenance point of view it is a good practice to keep different types of extension groups in some logical format. In this example, we are keeping our extensions limited to three digits, but our groups as four digits, using numbers in the 2000-2999 range for ring groups, and numbers in the 4000-4999 range for call queues. This is done purely for ease of maintenance.

A little bit of planning for our extensions will go a long way towards the success of our deployment and prevent changing people's extensions later on, as that can be a costly endeavor when we have a large number of users. For most deployments of TrixBox, we won't generally go above four digits with three being the most common setup. We must also consider our growth and any upcoming, foreseeable, major changes to the company. For example, if we know we will be expanding into new territories soon, or if there is a large merger on the horizon, we will have to consider how our phone system may change at that point.

The following table lays out a simple method for recording the information on extension numbers and recording the important information about the user. We should record:

- Display name (also used in the company directory)
- Extension number
- Outbound caller-id (this will override other caller-id settings)
- Record incoming/outgoing calls (on-demand, always, or never)
- Extension password (this is for the device, not for voicemail)

Name	Extension	Outbound Caller-ID	Record Calls	Password
Joe Smith	300	555-1212	Always	300
John Taylor	301	555-1213	Always	301

For extensions that will also have voicemail, we will also need the following information:

- Voicemail password
- Email address (optional, notifications, and attachments)
- Pager email address (optional, for short notifications)
- Email attachment yes/no (if set to yes, a .wav file will be emailed to the recipient)
- Play caller-id yes/no (if set to yes, caller-id will be read prior to the message)
- Play envelope yes/no (if set to yes, date and time will be read prior to the message)
- Delete voicemail yes/no (if set to yes, voicemail will be deleted after it is emailed)
- Voicemail context (this is used to group people into separate isolated groups such as having multiple companies hosted on the same PBX system)

Ring Groups

A **ring group** is a group of extensions that can all be made to ring at the same time when a single extension is called. This can be a useful feature within an organization as it allows the nearest available user to answer the phone.

If the inbound call volume to a given group of users does not exceed the capacity of the group to handle the calls, then a ring group is a good solution as it will immediately ring through all the available extensions that are assigned to it, thus minimizing the wait time before a caller is sent to an agent. With Asterisk PBX, an outside phone number can actually be a part of a ring group that can be used, for example, to ring our extension and our cell phone at the same time. However, we may need to play with the timing setting to prevent the voicemail of the outside line from picking up the call.

Ring groups can be configured as 'ring all', or 'hunt'. When configured as ring all the incoming call will ring at each extension simultaneously, whereas a hunt group will try ringing each extension individually.

Let us record the important information relating to the ring groups in the table that follows. We should record the following:

- The name of the group
- The number assigned to this group
- The ring strategy of the group (a ring all or a hunt group)
- The audio announcement to be played
- The prefix for the caller-id
- The destination to route a call if no one is available (to voicemail or to an operator for example)
- The extensions that are members of this group

Group Name	Group #	Ring Strategy	Announcement	CID Prefix	N/A Destination	Members
Sales	2000	Ring All	sales_greet	Sales	VM300	202, 205, 207, 209
Support	2001	Hunt	support_start	Spt	VM310	250, 251, 252, 253

Call Queues

The **call queue** is one of the most advanced features of Asterisk and yet is still fairly simple to implement, thanks to the FreePBX interface. Previously available only in high-end phone systems, the call queue is a standard feature of Asterisk PBX.

A call queue is different from a ring group in that the caller is not sent immediately to all the available agents. When a caller is sent to a call queue, they are sent to a virtual holding area to wait for the next available agent. During the wait, they can be listening to music on-hold and be told their position in the queue and the estimated hold time. Call queues are extremely valuable in sales and support organizations where inbound call volume can sometimes exceed the number of available agents. This provides a level of additional call capacity to the company while assuring the caller that they will be taken care of in the order that they called in, rather than having to continually call back.

For example, a support organization may only have five technicians. However, if a sixth call comes in, somebody would have to pick up the call and manually put the caller on hold. This becomes a real nightmare if even more calls become stacked up. With a call queue, additional callers are automatically put on hold and are answered in the order that they called.

When we call our telephone company or other organizations for support, we experience the call queue. We are often greeted with messages such as "*We are experiencing high call volumes at present, you are being held in a queue. We will deal with your enquiry shortly*". When planning call queues we should consider what we want the callers to hear, how much wait callers can tolerate, and how many agents we need online at a particular time. When planning our queues, we should record:

- A unique name for the queue
- A unique number to identify the queue
- A password for access to the queue
- The announcement to be played to the caller periodically
- Category of hold music to be played
- Ring strategy
- Static members of the queue

Queue Name	Queue #	Password	Announcement	On-Hold Music Category	Ring Strategy	Static Agents
Sales	2000		Sales_queue	Default	ringall	202, 205, 207,209
Support	2001		Support_queue	Default	ringall	250, 251, 252, 253

Agents

Agents go hand-in-hand with the call queues to determine who the next caller in the queue gets passed to. With the call queues, there are two ways to handle agents. Agents can either be given an extension and a password to dial to cause them to "log in" to the queue or certain extensions can be placed into a static agent list and will always ring regardless of whether or not an agent chooses to log in or not.

Connectivity

Once we know how many users we will have, we need to figure out the maximum number of concurrent phone calls we might receive at any time. This will determine the type of connectivity we will need for our system. The second part of this is to determine what percentage of the calls are outbound calls and how many of our outbound calls are long distance calls.

PSTN

The most basic PSTN connection is a POTS (Plain Old Telephone Service) line. A POTS line is the normal analog circuit that we have in our house. Small companies may just have a handful of POTS lines coming into their phone system.

Digium is currently the primary source of hardware cards to enable PSTN connectivity and it has different cards capable of supporting 1 to 24 POTS lines.

The most basic form of connectivity is a standard analog phone line. Digum's TDM400P is a multi-port card that when populated with FXO modules can support up to 4 analog phone lines per card while the TDM2400 can support up to 24 analog lines.

Using FXO modules will work fine for smaller installations. However, if we need more lines the next step is to move into a voice T1 line. By utilizing a T1 line, the phone calls are multiplexed over only a few actual wires enabling up to 23 phone lines per T1. By using Digium's single, dual, or quad port T1 cards, we can easily enable up to 92 phone lines. In some areas, an interim step between POTS lines and a full T1 is ISDN service. We should contact our telephone service company to see what types of circuits are available at our location.

The following chart will help us match PSTN connectivity options with different types of cards:

Lines	Card	Number of Cards
1-2	X100P	2
1-2	TDM400P	1 (2 FXS Modules)
3-4	TDM4001	1 (4 FXS Modules)
6-8	TDM4001	2 (4 FXS Modules)
1-24	TDM2400	1 (6 FXS Modules)
1-24	TE110P	1 (1 T1 Line)
25-48	TE205P	1 (2 T1 Lines)
49-96	TE405P	1 (4 T1 Lines)

VoIP

Just because Asterisk works exceptionally well with Internet Service Providers, it doesn't mean that we have to use them. For many companies, using regular phone circuits provides the reliability that they have come to rely upon over the years. It may also be difficult to port the existing phone numbers over to an Internet Telephone Service Provider.

VoIP connectivity is among the many things that makes Asterisk such a compelling solution. By using internet services, some companies can realize substantial cost savings over regular PSTN lines.

Using Voice over Internet Protocol (VoIP), phone calls can be placed over a broadband connection using Internet Telephone Service Providers (ITSPs). These ITSPs connect our VoIP phone call to the PSTN. For the most part, ITSPs are the most economical telephone connectivity available. With prices ranging from 1.2 to 2.0 cents per minute, no monthly fees, and no long distance charges, companies that are used to paying huge phone bills can realize a dramatic cost savings.

The bandwidth usage of an ITSP will vary dramatically based upon the codec we will use. The following chart outlines the most common codecs and their bandwidth utilization:

Codec	Single Call	Two Calls	Additional Calls	Calls per megabit
G.711 (ulaw)	81.1kbps	148.0 kbps	65.9kbps	15
ILBC	28.0 kbps	49.3 kbps	21.2 kbps	47
G.729	30.0 kbps	39.7 kbps	9.6kbps	103
GSM	35.4 kbps	50.2 kbps	14.7 kbps	68

While there are many more codecs available, these represent the most common ones that are in use today. G.729 is one of the most preferred codecs especially for remote users. However, to use G.729 within TrixBox we will need to purchase a G.729 license that will cost us about $10 per channel that it is used on.

When compared to a voice T1 or PRI that can handle 24 voice lines, G.711, which is one of the most common codecs for VoIP providers, can handle about 21 concurrent conversations on a data T1 (1.5 MBs) whereas the remaining codecs offer a dramatic increase in capacity over standard voice circuits. There is a trade-off, however. The more compression we use, the more CPU power is required. For example, running 100 channels using the G.729 codec could put quite a drain on the resources available in our PBX system. Thorough testing of our system before rolling it out is critical to ensure that the hardware has the capacity to cope with the load that will be placed upon it.

As you can see, the local area network requirements are minimal at best and a regular 100 MB network can handle a large number of telephone conversations, before you need to expand the network. As the availability of broadband at higher speeds has become more prevalent, bandwidth requirements are becoming less of an issue. However, we must still ensure that we have planned adequately and that we are not overloading the network causing degradation in service.

ITSPs

There are dozens of different Internet Telephone Service Providers around with a large number of options, calling plans, prices, and services. Choosing the best one for our needs can be a frustrating exercise, if we don't plan in advance exactly what we are looking for.

If we are using PSTN for our inbound lines, we may only want to have some VoIP lines for outbound calls for extra capacity, failover, or even to save on long distance or international calls. Some companies find that by using ITSPs, they can reduce the number of PSTN lines, which can result in a substantial cost savings per month, not including the reduction in cost of the long distance fees.

Some ITSPs provide only outbound calling connections while others provide both outbound terminations as well as inbound DID numbers. This can also be a very inexpensive means of getting a toll-free number for our company. Along with the different types of service, we will also need to choose between pre-pay, pay-as-we-go, and unlimited pricing plans. Before making a final decision on an ITSP we should research them fully, get references, and read some reviews. Right now ITSPs come and go; so, we should make sure we find one with a proven track record.

A final consideration for choosing an ITSP will be the codecs that they support. If we're planning a large number of VoIP lines, we may want to consider a provider that supports G.729 and purchase the correct number of licenses for the number of channels we will be using. A list of service providers is available on the Asterisk Wiki at http://www.voip-info.org/wiki-VOIP+Service+Providers.

DID Lines (Direct Inward Dial)

DID, or Direct Inward Dial, is simply the phone number that is dialled to make our phone ring. Usually, a POTS line will only have a single DID assigned to it. However, we can have numerous DID numbers on a T1/PRI line. For ITSPs that provide DID numbers, most of them will provide any number of DID numbers on our connection. We should also determine which departments and individuals in our company need their own direct phone numbers during the planning stage of our deployment.

When planning our DID requirements, we should take into account the following:

- The name we will give to the trunk (usually the name of the provider and a number if we have more than one trunk from the same provider)
- The technology in use (which protocol/line-type we are using for connecting to our provider)
- How many channels this particular trunk provides
- The order in which these trunks will be used for outbound calls

Trunk Name	Technology	Channels	DID	Outbound Order
SBC T1	PRI	23	949-231-1300 - 949-231-1500	2
Teliax	IAX	10	949-679-8555	1
PSTN-1	PSTN	4	949-679-1800 - 949-679-1804	3

Telephones

When it comes to the user experience, we should consider our telephone requirements carefully. While the more technical users will be able to handle most hard and soft phones in their stride, there may be a requirement for some user training for many of our users. Thus, we should evaluate the available options carefully.

Hard Phones

One of the advantages of Asterisk PBX is its ability to use any SIP-compliant telephone device. Good quality hard phones can be purchased for well under $100US. Phones like the Grandstream GXP-2000 have been on sale for as little as $85US and contain business functions like four lines, multiple speed-dial buttons, call-transfer button, call-conference button, backlit LCD display, and numerous other features.

Other major manufacturers include Linksys, Cisco, Snome, Zultys, and Polycom just to name a few.

Along with the standard desk phones, new Wifi phones take advantage of wireless networks and connect directly over the network back to the PBX.

The final type of hard phone is a regular analog phone. While we can't plug a regular phone directly into our Asterisk PBX, we can use an analog telephone adapter (ATA) or a channel bank to connect regular POTS phones into our system.

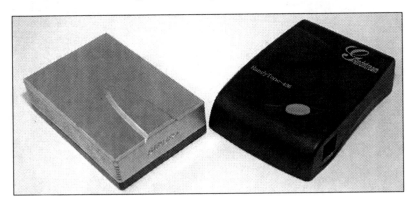

Soft Phones

Soft phones, as the name implies are software-based phones. These are programs that run on our computer and work like a normal extension to our PBX using microphone and speakers. There are a number of freely available soft phones that work under Windows, Mac OSX, and Linux. The ones listed below will run on all of these systems, although there are others that will run on only one or two of these OSs.

- SJLabs SJPhone: `http://sjlabs.com`

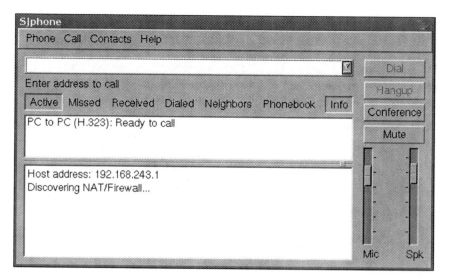

- Counterpath X-Lite: http://counterpath.com

- IDEFISK: http://asteriskguru.com/idefisk

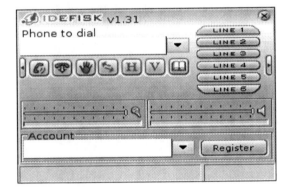

IVR (Interactive Voice Response)

The Digital Receptionist menu within the FreePBX interface provides for Interactive Voice Response (IVR) menus. A well designed IVR system is one of the key features that can give a company a very professional appearance. An example of an IVR menu would go like this:

"Thank you for calling American Widgets, for sales press 1, for support press 2, for a company directory press the pound key, or you may dial an extension at any time"

TrixBox's FreePBX interface allows us to easily build complex, multi-branching voice menus to help route callers to appropriate departments. For example, once a user presses "2" for support, another menu will ask the user to *"press 1 for the Presidio model line, press 2 for the Pendleton model line"*.

Using the IVR menu system, we can route any valid key sequence to another menu, to a voicemail address, to an extension, or even to a custom application.

Designing our IVR menus in advance will give everyone a chance to chime in on exactly how the phone system should work and then it becomes a roadmap to the actual programming. The following diagram demonstrates a typical IVR menu design:

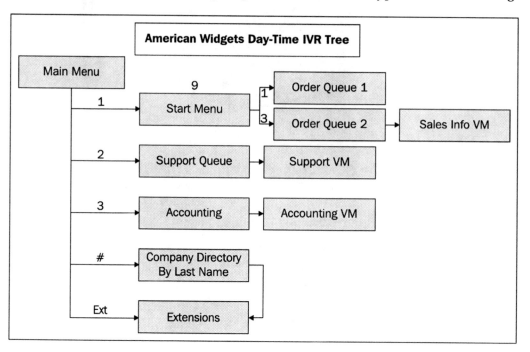

It is frustrating to call a company and get a poorly designed IVR menu. The IVR menu is the first interaction a caller has with the company, and a bad IVR design will leave a lasting negative impression on the caller. When designing our IVR, we need to think in terms of the caller and what they may want, not necessarily what we may want.

Following are a few general rules to keep in mind when designing our system:

- Keep it simple: Some experts claim that most people remember things in groups of three. With this in mind, designing a menu with 8 or 9 options is probably not a wise move. Separate logical groups into submenus if possible, to keep the number of options to a minimum.

- Don't play "Find the Human": There might be times when the best designed automated system will fail to give somebody the answer they are looking for. Always give callers the option to get to a live person. Nothing is more frustrating than being in a closed IVR system with no way out. Often, people will start trying extension numbers in hopes of reaching a person that can forward them to someone that can actually assist them.

- Don't ask for useless information: I won't mention any names, but one company I call on a regular basis asks me to enter my cell phone number and the last four digits of my social security number. While that is all well and good, I have to repeat this exact information to whoever finally answers the phone. If I have to say it to the operator, what was the point of asking me for it before?

- Let me go back: If the caller accidentally makes a mistake, make sure they have the option of moving back to the previous menu. After all, callers are human and will make mistakes sometimes. There is no need to make them pay for their mistake by having to wade through even more menus or having to hang up and call back.

- System Recordings: When deciding how to set up our system, we should plan out our system recordings carefully. The best laid out IVR system will become an embarrassment if the voice recordings do not sound clear and professional. Consider professional recording in the absence of anyone good enough for voice recording. There are a number of services available that will provide top quality voice talent at reasonable rates.

When planning the layout of our IVR system we should note each entry with:

- The name of the menu
- The selection number relating to that command
- The destination this command takes us to (queue, ring group, extension, another menu etc.)

IVR Name	Selection	Destination
Main	1	Sales RG
Main	2	Support Queue
Main	3	Accounting IVR
Accounting	1	Ext 200
Payroll	2	Ext 201

Fax Requirements

While scanning and emailing is becoming easier and therefore more popular, nearly every company still has a fax machine. With TrixBox and appropriate hardware, we can route inbound faxes to either an extension that has a fax machine attached to it, or to a particular email address. In a simple scenario, it is sometimes easiest to bypass the PBX altogether and have dedicated POTS lines connected to fax machines.

Case Studies

We will now take a look at applying some of these layouts to some simple case studies.

American Widgets Consulting Services

AWCS is a full service IT consulting business in southern California. With a small office and several technicians out in the field all day, communication is a key requirement to keep the technicians informed and provide service in the office. One big requirement was to try to cut down on very high cell phone bills. The sales people needed their extensions as well as their cell phones to ring and managers wanted extensions at home.

This is a great candidate for TrixBox as the package contained every feature the company wanted.

They decided to go with three digit extension numbers, to use VoIP for internal calls as much as possible, and to have a few external lines connected as individual POTS lines.

- Extensions: Three digits.
- Ring groups: Small number of employees; so all incoming generic numbers could probably ring at all employee desks.
- Call queues: No queues; if no one is available go directly to voicemail.

- Connectivity:
    - ◦ PSTN: Less than 5 lines, one for each employee and one generic number to be used for sales and support calls.
    - ◦ VOIP: SIP and IAX connectivity.
    - ◦ ITSP: One or two ITSPs to provide some redundancy; most calls are likely to be from employee to employee, to cut down on call costs for roaming users.
- Telephones:
    - ◦ Hard phones: One per desk.
    - ◦ Soft phones: One for each user on their laptop and/or desktop.
- IVR (Interactive Voice Response): A very simple menu system, which allows dialing an extension directly or calling support/sales.
- Fax requirements: Single separate fax line.

The company could also use SugarCRM for tracking clients and jobs.

International Widgets Call Centers Ltd

IWCC is a medium sized company with a single call center which employs about 50 people with 30 agents on the lines making and receiving calls at the same time. It also has a few small departments for HR, IT, and Accounts.

Their requirements could be met as follows:

- Extensions: Three digits.
- Ring groups: A ring group for each department (IT/Accounts/HR/etc.), each set to 'ring all' on a group of two to four extensions.
- Call Queues: Each client or internal calling campaign would have its own queue and clients could be billed based on calls handled from those queues.
- Connectivity:
    - ◦ PSTN: The call center would require a large number of lines, probably around 1.2 lines per agent as they would expect all their calling staff to be on calls at the same time, as well as leaving room for the other departments to make and receive external calls.
    - ◦ VOIP: SIP and IAX connectivity.

- ○ ITSP: At least three or four ITSPs with redundancy configured between them all. Likewise, they would also require ITSPs that have cheap rates, to access the PSTN in the countries they make calls to in order to decrease operating costs for any calling that occurs internationally.

- Telephones:
  - ○ Hard phones: One per desk for the IT/HR/ Accounts departments.
  - ○ Soft phones: One for each agent employed to handle the queues.

- IVR (Interactive Voice Response): Possibly multiple IVR systems for incoming call campaigns as well as an IVR for clients calling in with sales or account issues, with each IVR having its own DID.

- Fax requirements: Depending on the nature of the calling campaigns with clients, the company may be required to handle incoming faxes or send faxes. There would also likely be a need for multiple fax lines.

We can see from the case studies above, that when we are planning a PBX system, we should answer these basic questions in order to simplify the process. If we take care to fill out the charts and tables when it comes to installing and configuring the system, we should have very little to question and it should be a matter of just inputting these values into the various forms provided by TrixBox.

Summary

In this chapter, we have seen how we can easily plan and lay out our system and had a look at gathering the requirements of a PBX through a couple of case studies. It would now be a good point to consider our own system, if we are currently building one. Then, in the following chapters, we can build the system accordingly.

5
Installing TrixBox

Now that we have a basic understanding of what TrixBox can do and have an adequate deployment plan, we can get started with the installation of the software. We will download the CD-ROM image, install it on our computer, and get prepared to start our initial configuration. In this chapter, we will cover the installation process, some basic system configuration, and the basic tools that are included in TrixBox.

Obtain the Software

TrixBox is available in a couple of formats. Firstly, there is the ISO image that can be burned to a CD and then installed. Secondly, we can download and install a `tar.gz` file to an existing CentOS system. The former method is by far the simplest and is what we will cover here. The ISO image can be downloaded by going to `http://www.trixbox.org` and clicking on the **download** link, or by going to the SourceForge project page directly at `http://sourceforge.net/project/showfiles.php?group_id=123387&package_id=192286&release_id=426959`.

We should download the latest version (avoiding any files marked as beta or alpha) of the ISO image to our computer and burn it to a blank CD with our favourite CD-burning software. The ISO is about 510 Mb in size, and may grow in future versions as well. We should ensure we have adequate space on our hard drive to download the file.

Installation

We start by putting the CD into the CD-ROM drive of the computer we will be installing TrixBox on, and then boot the computer ensuring that we have configured it to boot from CD-ROM. We will be presented with a start-up screen with several options:

```
   -  To install trixbox, press the <ENTER> key.

Warning: This will format your hard drive and destroy
all existing data on your computer!!

   -  Use the function keys listed below for more information.

[F1-Main] [F2-Options] [F3-General] [F4-Kernel] [F5-Rescue]
boot: _
```

The advanced options that we can access here can be skipped for most installations. However, it is often good to do a media check beforehand as this checks the CD for errors and helps us to ensure that the system will install without errors. Advanced options can be accessed by pressing the following buttons:

- *F1* brings us to the main screen (the one shown in the previous screenshot).

- *F2* takes us to the options menu that allows us to run a media check and a memory test.

- *F3* gives us some more information and options for modifying the screen resolution as the system boots. This can usually be ignored.

- *F4* gives information on additional kernel parameters that we can pass to the kernel, if we are having problems while booting.

- *F5* shows us the rescue option that can be used to repair our system after installation, if we are having difficulties while booting into TrixBox.

Media Check

We can perform a media check by pressing *F2*, which lists the options we have, although most of these aren't useful for our installation. We can see that a media check is run by typing `linux mediacheck`. This takes a few minutes and helps prevent frustrating media errors during the installation process.

Doing so will show us some boot messages and after a minute or two we should see:

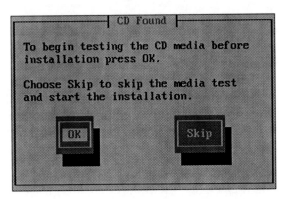

If we press *Enter* with the **OK** box highlighted, we should then see the following screen:

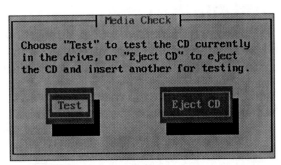

Pressing *Enter* with the **Test** button highlighted begins the test, which shows a progress bar. We need not worry about it referring to a **CentOS-4 i386 DVD**; this is due to the fact that TrixBox is derived from CentOS, which has a DVD version.

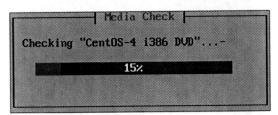

If the check is successful, we should see the following screen:

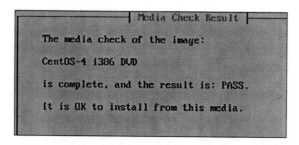

This means that we had no errors in the CD-burning process and that we have a valid CD to install from. Since the TrixBox installation is automated and requires little user input, the most common errors are due to the CD-ROM being burned with errors. If we see anything other than the preceding screenshot, or if it indicates a **FAIL**, we should burn the CD again and ensure our burning software verifies that the burn was successful.

After pressing *Enter* on this screen, we will be asked if we want to test another disk. TrixBox only has a single disk so we can ignore this, by pressing the right arrow followed by *Enter* to continue with the installation.

Automated Installation

At the initial boot screen, if we press *Enter*, we will go straight into the automated installation. However, if we do the media check, as explained in the previous section, we will eventually go into the automated installation after performing the check.

First, we will be prompted for our keyboard layout. We can scroll up and down with the arrow keys and use the *space bar* or *Enter* to select options in the following screen:

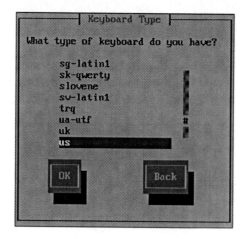

At this point, the installer checks for any valid hard drives in the system. There are rare occasions when some hard drives, particularly SCSI or SATA drives, are not recognized.

Next, we are prompted for a password for the root user. It is advisable not to forget this password as we will need it to log into our system when it is up and running.

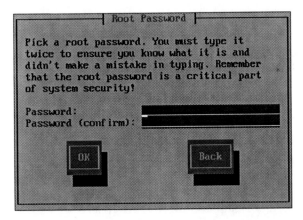

We will also be prompted to enter our time zone information:

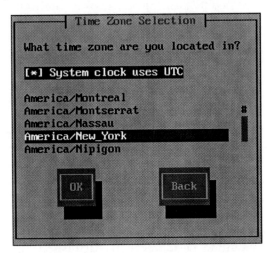

The setup will format the hard drive in the computer and install the operating system and all the related files.

[Warning: This will erase all the information on the
computer. Do not do this on any machine that contains
valuable data on its hard drive.]

We will see a few progress bars and other information on screen, which we can ignore as the rest of the installation is automated. The process can take a while depending on the specifications of the machine we are using. It can take anywhere from a few minutes to an hour or so.

When the initial setup is complete, the installer will eject the CD and reboot. When the system boots back again, it will begin compiling and setting up all the additional software and tools that are part of the TrixBox system.

Once the final configuration is complete, the system will reboot once again and present us with a login screen on the console containing the following text:

```
CentOS release 4.3 (Final)
Kernel 2.6.9-22.EL on an i686
asterisk1 login:
```

TrixBox is now completely installed and ready to use. We can log in here as the user root with the password we entered during the setup process.

Once we log in, we will be given some additional information:

```
Welcome to TrixBox
For access to the TrixBox web GUI use this URL
http://192.168.1.5
For help on TrixBox commands we can use from this
command shell type help-TrixBox.
[root@asterisk1 ~]#
```

[**SSH Access**

When we complete the TrixBox installation, we can also
access this console by SSH (Secure Shell). We can do this
by connecting to the address, for example ssh 192.168.1.5,
or by inputting the address into a GUI-based SSH client
like PuTTy (`http://www.chiark.greenend.org.uk/`
`~sgtatham/putty/`). There is also a Java SSH client which
we shall see later in this chapter.]

Assuming we had the correct date and time set in our computer's BIOS, we will only need to adjust the time zone setting. However, if the IP address that the system came up with is not what we want to use, then we will need to change that as well.

From the command prompt, type `setup` and hit *Enter*.

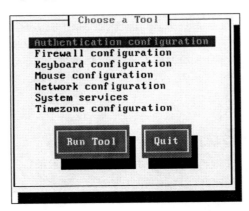

Select the **Network configuration** option to get into the TCP/IP properties screen.

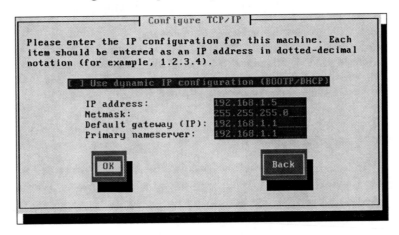

While we can use an automatically assigned IP address from a DHCP server, it is recommended to use a static IP address, which will make it easier to manage for any firewall settings and will prevent the IP address from changing and losing connectivity to the phones. Once we have set the network settings, we press the *Tab* button until the **OK** button is highlighted and then press *Enter* or the space bar. This drops us back to the configuration screen. We should then select the **Quit** button, which will put us back at the command line. If we type `reboot` at the prompt, the server will reboot so that the new settings can take effect.

Basic System Configuration

We will now have a look at some of the basic system management tools that we can use before we go on to configure the telephone functionality in the next chapter. There are some basic settings and updates we will want to take care of to make sure our system is up-to-date. If our system is on a public IP address, these settings are even more important to ensure that we have all the latest security updates. Regardless of what we may have heard, Linux operating systems have just as many security holes as Microsoft's operating systems and have to be patched on a regular basis. TrixBox is just another Linux server and in most circumstances should be treated as such.

Updating TrixBox

In most systems, keeping the system updated with all the latest operating-system patches and application updates requires maintaining long scripts and knowing obscure system commands to get the updates. With TrixBox, this is all handled by one simple command, the `trixbox-update.sh` script. This script can be run from the command prompt and will download and install any component that needs to be upgraded. Following is an example of using this script alongwith the output:

```
[root@asterisk1 ~]# trixbox-update.sh update
Installed: munin.noarch 0:1.2.4-7 munin-node.noarch 0:1.2.4-7 perl-
DateManip.noarch 0:5.42a-3 perl-HTML-Template.noarch 0:2.8-1.2.el4.
rf perl-Net-Server.noarch 0:0.93-1.el4.rf perl-rrdtool.i386 0:1.0.50-
3.2.el4.rf rrdtool.i386 0:1.0.50-3.2.el4.rf
Complete!
done.
Please reboot by typing reboot
```

The TrixBox script also updates itself so you may be asked if you want to replace the script during the upgrade process. If this occurs, type Y and press *Enter*, and later re-run the `trixbox-update.sh` script.

SMTP Server Setup

SMTP is the protocol that is used to send email. If we plan on using the voicemail-to-email feature and we are on a public IP address with no restrictions, we should be able to bypass this section. However, many places now require that all outbound email goes through our ISP's mail server to prevent spamming and email attacks. If we are in this situation, a few tweaks to the `sendmail` settings will get us up and running.

Firstly, we run the `setup-mail` script where we will be prompted to enter a hostname for our PBX.

```
[root@asterisk1 ~]# setup-mail
```

Usually, all we need to do is edit the `/etc/sendmail.cf` file and add our ISP's mail server information. For this, we will use the `nano` text file editor.

```
[root@asterisk1 ~]# nano /etc/mail/sendmail.cf
```

This will open the file in the editor:

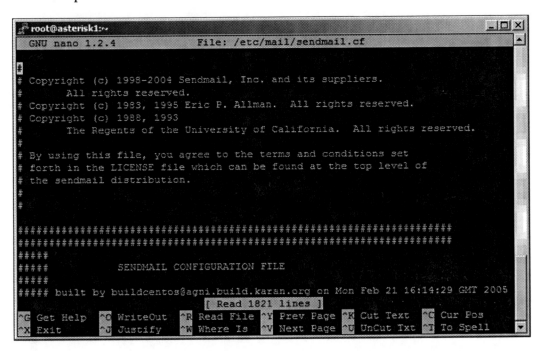

Use *Ctrl+w* to start the search function; enter `ds`, and hit *Enter*.

You want to find the line that looks like the following:

```
# "Smart" relay host (may be null)
DS
```

Edit the relay host to match our ISP's settings. For example, if we are using Cox Internet in California, we would use `smtp.west.cox.net` as shown here:

```
# "Smart" relay host (may be null)
DSsmtp.west.cox.net
```

Use *Ctrl+o* to save the changes and then *Ctrl+x* to exit. Reboot the server for the change to take effect.

The Web Interface

Besides the updates and mail configuration that we have seen, we can manage our server from the web interface easily. There are many different areas that we can access from here and the majority of our system configuration can be done within this nicely laid out and user-friendly web interface.

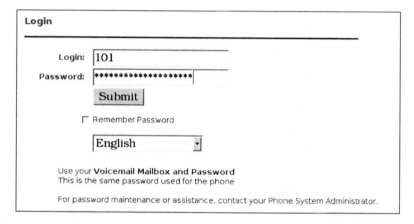

The web interface can be accessed by pointing the browser to the URL we were shown earlier when we logged into the text console (http://192.168.1.5 in this example). If we do not remember it, we will need to login again and it will be displayed.

After typing the URL, we will be greeted by the TrixBox main menu:

In the following sections, we will discuss each of the features that appear on the TrixBox main menu.

Voicemail and Recordings (ARI)

The Asterisk Recording Interface (ARI) is the repository of recorded sound files, including voicemails and recorded phone calls. Logging in with our extension number and voicemail password will give us access to all the recordings in our profile.

From ARI, we can also listen to, delete, and forward existing messages. Once we log in, we will see a list of our available recordings with the date of the recording, the time at which it was recorded, the caller-id of the originating call, the original mailbox the message was stored in, the duration of the recording, and a link to open a media player to listen to the recording.

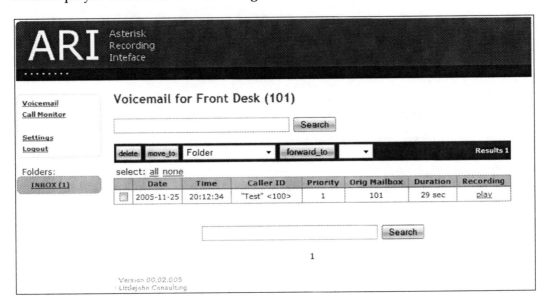

SugarCRM

The **Customer Relationship Management (CRM)** system that is included with TrixBox is **SugarCRM**. The **SugarCRM** package is a complete CRM package for managing customer contacts, leads, sales, etc. **SugarCRM** is the leading open-source CRM package and has some nice integration with Asterisk PBX for one-click dialling from the contact manager. **SugarCRM** is quite a large piece of software and we will cover it in more detail in Chapter 9.

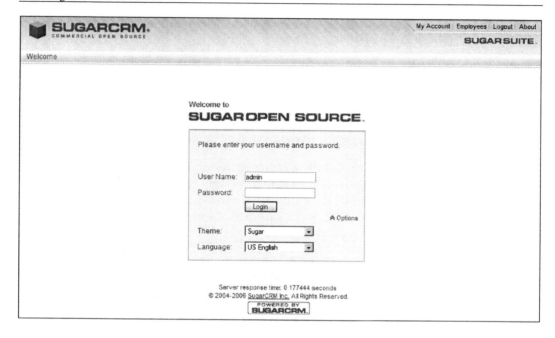

Flash Operator Panel

If we are going to have a receptionist that handles a large number of phone calls, the **Flash Operator Panel** can make managing incoming calls much easier. The **Flash Operator Panel** not only allows us to view the status of all of the extensions, queues, and trunks, but also we can transfer calls around by dragging and dropping. The following screenshot is an example of what we would see from a configured system. The **Flash Operator Panel** will be blank until we have configured our trunks, extensions, and queues.

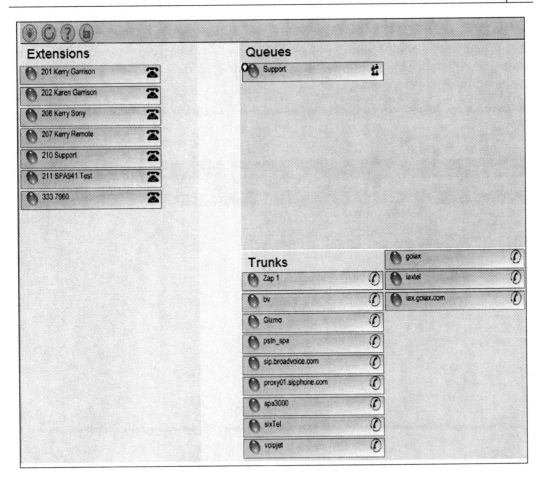

Web MeetMe Control

Built into TrixBox is the MeetMe Conference Room System in which every extension can create and manage its own conference rooms. The **Web MeetMe Control** is a web interface that allows a manager to see who is in the conference and mute, unmute, or kick users from a conference.

| Web MeetMe Control | | 8201 | | Connect | | November 25, 2005 |

	ID	Channel	ConfNo	Mode	
"Karen Garrison"	1	SIP/202-2cf3	8201	UnMuted	[MUTE] - [KICK]
"Kerry Garrison" (Admin)	2	SIP/201-0fcb	8201	UnMuted	[MUTE] - [KICK]

- Conference Users : [ROOM : 8201] -

1 / 1

System Administration

Clicking on the **System Administration** link from the TrixBox main menu will display another set of tools to help us manage our system. The following sections briefly describe these tools.

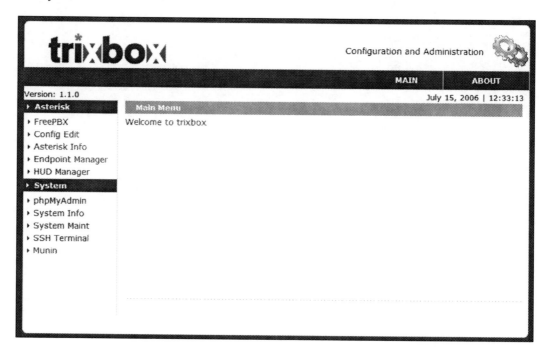

FreePBX

FreePBX is the primary management interface for managing users, extensions, ring groups, queues, trunks, and more. This is where we will spend the majority of our time configuring the system. We will need to get our system up and running before being able to use the other applications that are included with the system.

Config Edit

This tool is used to manually edit the actual config files. This is handy for making quick edits without having to log into the console or having to log in via an SSH session, although manual edits can be problematic if we don't follow the FreePBX conventions. However, this should only be done in case of urgency.

phpconfig for Asterisk PBX

/etc/asterisk /var/www/html/panel   /etc   /tftpboot Re-Read Configs

a2billing.conf

agents.conf

alarmreceiver.conf

applications.conf

asterisk.conf

cdr_mysql.conf

codecs.conf

dnsmgr.conf

dundi.conf

enum.conf

extconfig.conf

extensions.conf

extensions_additional.conf

extensions_custom.conf

extensions_hud.conf

extensions_trixbox.conf

features.conf

festival.conf

iax.conf

iax_additional.conf

iaxprov.conf

indications.conf

Asterisk Info

The **Asterisk Info** tool displays an information screen about our Asterisk installation for troubleshooting purposes.

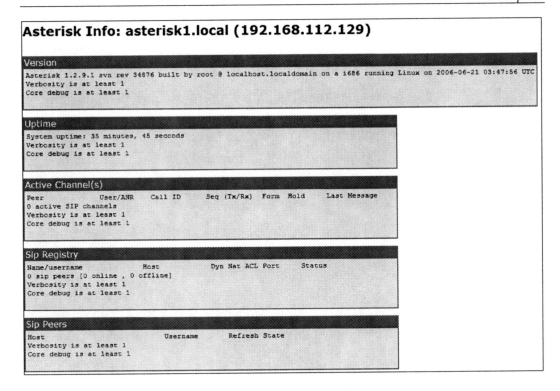

Endpoint Manager

This tool is used to create config files for telephone devices. Currently only Cisco phones are supported. In the future, tools for Polycom, Linksys, and Snom phones will be available.

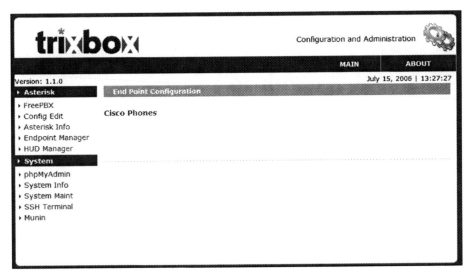

HUD Manager

The HUD Manager tool is used to configure the Fonality Heads-Up-Display tool. The server component will need to be installed separately.

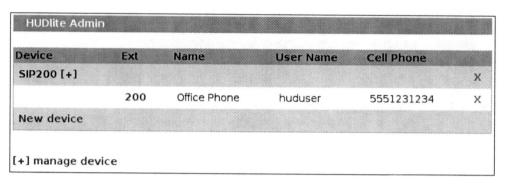

System Tools

There are various configuration tools that we can use for managing the server and the back-end process running on it.

phpMyAdmin

This is a tool to help us manage MySQL databases. The SugarCRM software, for example, is very SQL dependant. Even some of the other applications, such as Asterisk, store information in databases.

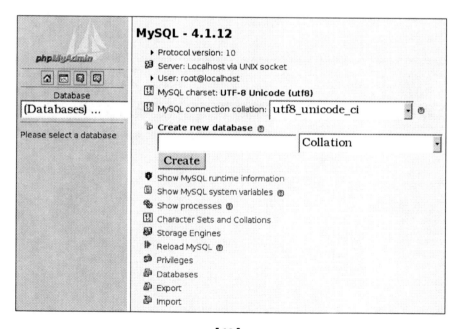

SQL skills and the use of phpMyAdmin are not within the scope of this book, but could be useful for any advanced troubleshooting. For further reading you can refer to the book *Mastering phpMyAdmin for Effective MySQL Management* from Packt Publishing (ISBN 1-904811-60-6).

System Info

The **System Info** tool displays a lot of useful information and statistics on our server, such as hostname, IP address information, and uptime.

System Vital	
Canonical Hostname	localhost
Listening IP	192.168.243.128
Kernel Version	2.6.9-34.0.1.EL
Distro Name	CentOS release 4.3 (Final)
Uptime	1 hours 30 minutes
Current Users	1
Load Averages	1.76 1.62 1.25

Information such as network statistics, which can be invaluable when checking for any network issues or to get an idea of how much bandwidth our server is using, is also displayed by this tool.

Network Usage			
Device	**Received**	**Sent**	**Err/Drop**
lo	530.61 KB	530.61 KB	0/0
eth0	155.69 KB	664.30 KB	0/0
sit0	0.00 KB	0.00 KB	0/0

Besides, the tool displays some specific details about the hardware in our system that can be very useful when trying to get support from other users or official support channels.

Hardware Information	
Processors	1
Model	Pentium III (Coppermine)
CPU Speed	847.62 MHz
Cache Size	256 KB
System Bogomips	1704.82
PCI Devices	- Bridge: Intel Corporation 82371AB/EB/MB PIIX4 ACPI
	- Ethernet controller: Advanced Micro Devices [AMD] 79c970 [PCnet32 LANCE]
	- Host bridge: Intel Corporation 440BX/ZX/DX - 82443BX/ZX/DX Host bridge
	- IDE interface: Intel Corporation 82371AB/EB/MB PIIX4 IDE
	- ISA bridge: Intel Corporation 82371AB/EB/MB PIIX4 ISA
	- Multimedia audio controller: Ensoniq ES1371 [AudioPCI-97]
	- PCI bridge: Intel Corporation 440BX/ZX/DX - 82443BX/ZX/DX AGP bridge
	- SCSI storage controller: BusLogic BT-946C
	- USB Controller: Intel Corporation 82371AB/EB/MB PIIX4 USB
	- VGA compatible controller: VMware Inc [VMware SVGA II] PCI Display Adapter
IDE Devices	- hda: VMware Virtual IDE Hard Drive (Capacity: 10.00 GB)
	- hdc: VMware Virtual IDE CDROM Drive

Finally, the tool displays memory and hard drive usage information, which we can use to determine the requirements of the server and how much capacity it is using.

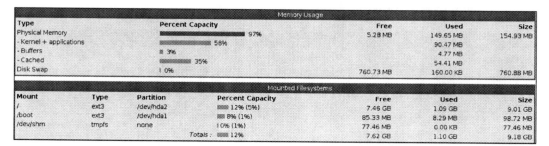

Memory Usage				
Type	Percent Capacity	Free	Used	Size
Physical Memory	97%	5.28 MB	149.65 MB	154.93 MB
- Kernel + applications	58%		90.47 MB	
- Buffers	3%		4.77 MB	
- Cached	35%		54.41 MB	
Disk Swap	0%	760.73 MB	160.00 KB	760.88 MB

Mounted Filesystems						
Mount	Type	Partition	Percent Capacity	Free	Used	Size
/	ext3	/dev/hda2	12% (5%)	7.46 GB	1.09 GB	9.01 GB
/boot	ext3	/dev/hda1	8% (1%)	85.33 MB	8.29 MB	98.72 MB
/dev/shm	tmpfs	none	0% (1%)	77.46 MB	0.00 KB	77.46 MB
			Totals : 12%	7.62 GB	1.10 GB	9.18 GB

System Maint

The **System maint** screen shows us the status of the Asterisk service as well as the cron (scheduling service), secure shell (SSH for remote login), and the web server (if this wasn't running we wouldn't be able to access this page!).

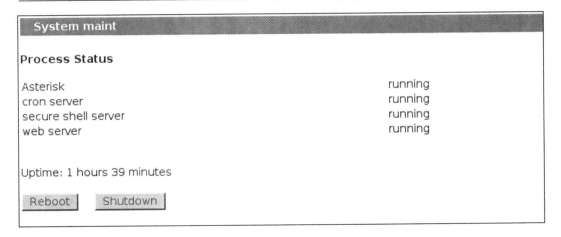

Process Status

Asterisk	running
cron server	running
secure shell server	running
web server	running

Uptime: 1 hours 39 minutes

Reboot   Shutdown

SSH Terminal

This is a Java SSH client used to log in to our server without having to have a keyboard and a monitor attached to our server. We can use this as if it were a local console, so we can run things like the update and setup scripts from within our web browser. When we have TrixBox up and running, we can stay in the web interface most of the time.

```
Login & password accepted
Last login: Tue Jul 11 06:04:16 2006

Welcome to trixbox
-----------------------------------------------------------

For access to the trixbox web GUI use this URL
http://192.168.112.129

For help on trixbox commands you can use from this
command shell type help-trixbox.

[root@asterisk1 ~]#
```

Connected to 192.168.112.129 ssh   online

Munin

Munin is a system monitoring tool to help us monitor the resources and performance of our server. Munin will create reports on system resources such as file-system usage, network traffic, processes, sendmail traffic, CPU usage, interrupts, memory usage, and many more. These can be invaluable in determining any bottlenecks on our server.

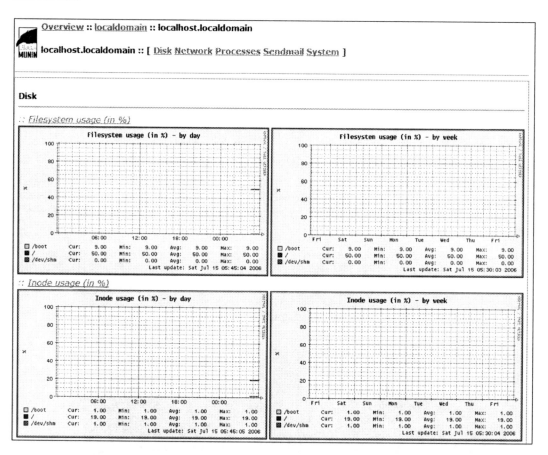

As can be seen in the screenshot, Munin gives us a more detailed information than the system info page we saw earlier. If we want to troubleshoot the server or do some capacity planning we should reference these graphs as they will give us a detailed breakdown of the server's performance.

Summary

In this chapter, we have taken a look at the installation of TrixBox and how to ensure its smooth functioning. We also had an overview of some of the basic system administration functions available to us in TrixBox. We have seen that there are a number of applications bundled with TrixBox, such as phpMyAdmin and SugarCRM, that offer us many more features than a simple telephony system.

6
TrixBox Configuration

The TrixBox system is up and running now and all the basic concepts have been understood. Hopefully, you have taken the time to design your IVR menus and have all your PSTN and VoIP connectivity options ready to go. In this chapter, you will learn to make the essential configurations for TrixBox. To get a basic system up and running, the following options will need to be configured:

- FreePBX
- Extensions
- Trunks
- Inbound routing
- Outbound routing
- Digital receptionist
- Ring groups
- Queues
- Music on-hold
- General settings

FreePBX

To get to the FreePBX administration page, we need to go to the TrixBox configuration web page:

If we click on the **System Administration** link, we will arrive at the following screenshot:

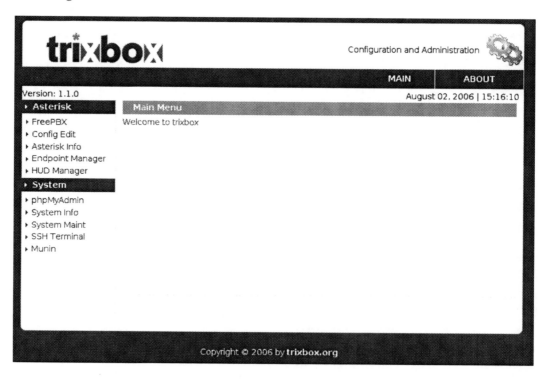

Clicking on the **FreePBX** link will prompt us for a username and password. The default login is **maint** with a password of **password**. Later on, we will see how to change these when we discuss securing our TrixBox server in Chapter 10.

Once we are logged in, we will be presented with the FreePBX main screen. From here, we can access many of the important Asterisk-related configurations and we will now have a walkthrough to set up some of the important telephony functions.

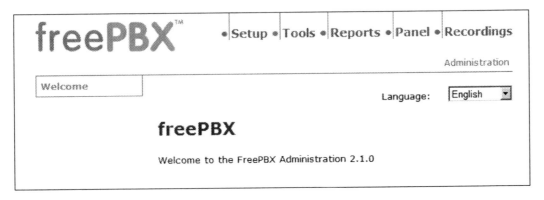

FreePBX has been designed to be modular and we can pick and choose which modules we want to turn on or off. The first thing we need to do is to set up the initial modules. Clicking on the **Tools** link, we select the modules we wish to use. For our first installation, we should go ahead and install all of them so we can see what each module can do.

There is also an online repository for new and updated modules. We can add additional functionality to our system with new modules and make sure we always have the latest modules by visiting the online repository on a regular basis.

Next, we will go through the different modules and see how they work and how to configure them. These modules will add in extra functionality to FreePBX so that we can configure the many different areas of our PBX.

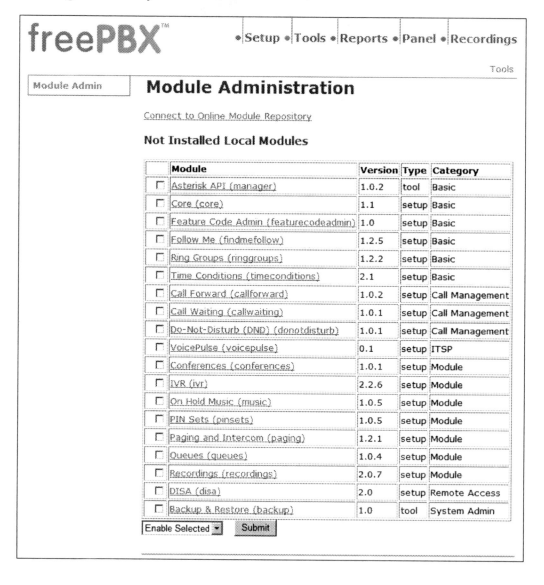

Extensions

As we saw in Chapter 4, a good design will go a long way towards a successful implementation. It is a good idea to lay out our extensions in a spreadsheet with all the relevant information. This will prevent us from having to go back and change extensions later on, if we find our numbering scheme not turning out the way we thought it would. If we fill in the spreadsheets as detailed in Chapter 4, they will come in very useful here.

In the FreePBX main menu, click the **Setup** link at the top of the screen and then select **Extensions** from the left-hand menu in the **Setup** page. This will bring up the main 'Extensions manager' screen. From here, we can add different types of extensions. Most VoIP phones today use the **SIP (Session Initiation Protocol)**, so this is the one we will probably use the most.

Some newer phones and ATA's (Analaog Telephone Adapter) also support the IAX2 protocol, which has the benefit of working much better behind firewalls. If we are going to have remote users, and if they can use IAX2, we will have far less problems than when using SIP.

Zap channels provide the ability to interface our Asterisk server to traditional PBX's and telephone equipment.

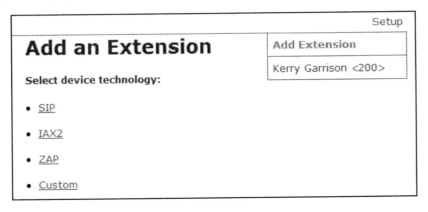

Our first goal is to make sure we can connect to the TrixBox server via an extension. So we will create a single extension for testing purposes, confirm everything is working, and then add additional extensions to ensure station-to-station connectivity. We can add a new extension by clicking on the **Extensions** link on the left-hand side menu bar of FreePBX menu and then clicking **Add Extension** on the top right. If we click on the **SIP** link, we will be able to access the menu shown in the following screenshot. For a basic extension, all we need is the **Extension Number**, **Display Name**, and **Secret** (password). We need to fill in this information, leave all other boxes at their defaults, and then click **Submit**.

Add SIP Extension

Add Extension

Extension Number: [   ]

Display Name: [   ]

Extension Options

Direct DID: [   ]

DID Alert Info: [   ]

Outbound CID: [   ]

Emergency CID: [   ]

Record Incoming: [On Demand ▼]

Record Outgoing: [On Demand ▼]

Device Options

secret [   ]

dtmfmode [rfc2833   ]

Voicemail & Directory: [Disabled ▼]

[Submit]

Once we have submitted the form and are sure about it, we need to click on the red bar at the top of the screen to apply our changes.

You have made changes - when finished, click here to APPLY them

freePBX • Setup • Tools • Reports • Panel • Recordings

Configuring our First Device

With our extension created, we now need to configure a device to talk to the Asterisk PBX. Any SIP device will do; but for a quick test, we will configure **Counterpath's** (`http://counterpath.com`) **X-Lite SoftPhone**. The first time we run X-Lite, it will open up the SIP Proxy settings for us to enter the server information. Using our server and extension information, configure X-Lite as follows (leaving any unmentioned options at their defaults):

Feature	Configuration
Enabled	**Yes**
Display Name	Any name
Username	Extension Number
Authorization User	Extension Number
Password	Extension Secret
Domain/Realm	Default
SIP Proxy	IP Address of Asterisk PBX

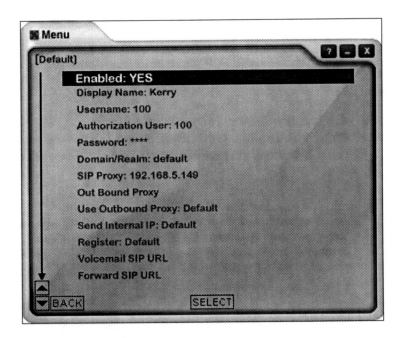

Once we have all the options set, close the windows and X-Lite will attempt to connect to our server. If everything is set properly, X-Lite will tell us that we are logged in and display our extension number.

If our phone has successfully registered with Asterisk PBX, type in ***65** and hit *Enter*. This will tell Asterisk to read back our current extension. If we hear the voice say *"Your extension is 100"*, then we are well on our way to getting our system fully operational.

If everything is working, we can set up a second extension and make sure the two extensions can call each other and that both sides can hear audio from the other side. We now have a working telephone system with extensions that can call each other!

> *65 is the number that is dialled in order to have our extension read back to us. We use this to ensure that we are using the correct phone and credentials. There are a variety of other shortcut numbers for use in Asterisk. We will cover each of these in the next chapter.

Basic Troubleshooting

When the phones and the server are on the same network subnet, there are very few things that can go wrong; usually, typos entering extension ids, passwords, and server IP addresses. For our first setup, it is not recommended to set up our phones on a different network than the server as this makes troubleshooting much harder. If we have double-checked all the extensions and X-Lite settings, and X-Lite still does not log in to the server, then we may have some networking issue. This can sometimes be solved by editing the extension on the server.

Editing Extensions

To edit an extension, we need to go back to the Extensions menu we were in previously. In the top-right corner, we should see the extensions we have added, similar to the following dialog box:

Add Extension
Barrie <200>
Kristina <201>
Cameron <202>
Logan <203>
Nathan <204>

We can edit by clicking on any one of these extensions. When we edit an extension, we will see a number of extra options that were not there when we initially set up the extension. These can be found under the **Device options** section.

Device Options	
secret	200
dtmfmode	rfc2833
canreinvite	no
context	from-internal
host	dynamic
type	friend
nat	never
port	5060
qualify	no
callgroup	
pickupgroup	
disallow	
allow	
dial	SIP/200
accountcode	
mailbox	200@device

On the line that reads **nat: never**, we need to change this to **nat: yes**. This can help resolve some networking issues and is mandatory for phones that are on a different subnet than the Asterisk server itself and those that are separated by NAT (Network Address Translation). The reason for this is that when using **Network Address Translation** protocol, IP addresses are dynamically remapped from a private IP space to the public IP space. If we experience issues such as one-way audio, it is almost always a sign that we are experiencing problems associated with NAT. By changing the setting to correctly match the remote device, we will almost certainly solve the problem. If the problem persists, then we may seek help from the online TrixBox forum at http://www.trixbox.org/modules/newbb/index.php.

Trunks

At this point, we have a basic PBX system running with internal extensions. Now, it's time to communicate with the outside world. If this is our first installation, we may not have any hardware to connect a phone line yet. So our first trunk is going to be a VoIP trunk.

Setting Up a VoIP Trunk

For our first trunk, we will walk through the configuration of **Free World Dialup**. This is an extremely common service used to test Asterisk functionality. We will first need to go to `http://www.freeworlddialup.com/` and register for a free account. Once we have our account information, we will need to log in to go to the **Extra Features** page. Be sure to activate IAX.

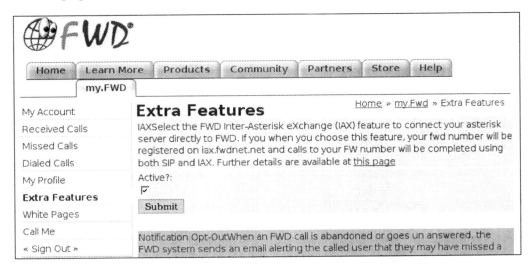

This will take about 10 minutes to take effect. In the meantime, we will configure the trunk on the server.

Trunk Setup

We will now create an IAX trunk to connect to the Free World Dialup account. Clicking on the **Trunks** link in the left-hand side of the FreePBX menu and then on the **Add IAX2 Trunk** link will display the screen shown overleaf. We need to configure it, replacing **Name** and **number** with our full name and the telephone number provided by Free World Dialup. The **4** relates to the maximum number of calls that can use this trunk at one time.

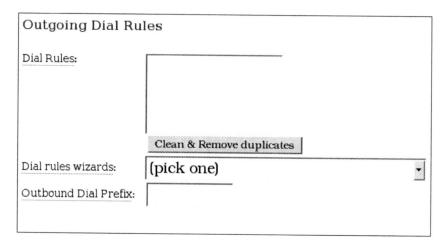

General Settings

Outbound Caller ID:	"Name" <number>
Maximum channels:	4

The **Outgoing Dial Rules** section doesn't require modification for this example; we will cover these rules later.

Outgoing Dial Rules

Dial Rules:

Clean & Remove duplicates

Dial rules wizards: (pick one)

Outbound Dial Prefix:

Outgoing Settings covers the options for outgoing calls as shown in the next screenshot. **Trunk Name** is a unique name for the trunk when used in other settings within FreePBX. For now, **fwd** is good but we should make it something more unique if we plan to have multiple Free World Dialup accounts on our system.

In the **PEER Details** box, we have the connection settings for connecting this trunk to the IAX service provided by Free World Dialup.

- **host=iax2fwdnet.net**: This should be entered verbatim, since it is the hostname of the IAX2 server provided by Free World Dialup.

- **secret=mypassword**: The **mypassword** string should be replaced with the password we set when registering with Free World Dialup.

- **type=peer**: This should be typed verbatim, since it tells Asterisk what sort of connection we want to establish with our provider.

- **username=myfwdnumber**: The string **myfwdnumber** should be replaced with the number provided by Free World Dialup.

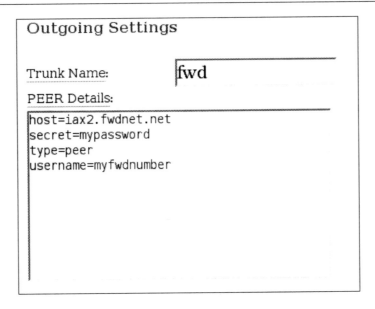

The settings for the **Incoming Settings** section shown overleaf should be entered verbatim. These allow incoming calls to be processed under the correct context.

The **USER Details** box has the following options:

- **allow**: This defines which codecs to allow.
- **auth**: This setting specifies what authentication method to use. FWD uses **rsa**, which is an algorithm for public-key encryption.
- **context**: The context tells the system how to handle incoming calls. By setting this to **from-pstn**, any incoming call from FWD will behave as if it was a call from a regular phone line.
- **disallow**: This option specifies which codecs to refuse. In our example, we are refusing all codecs and then only allowing **ulaw**.
- **inkeys**: FWD uses a key file for authentication. This key is provided with current versions of Asterisk.
- **type**: Since we are initiating calls into the system, the type here is **user**.

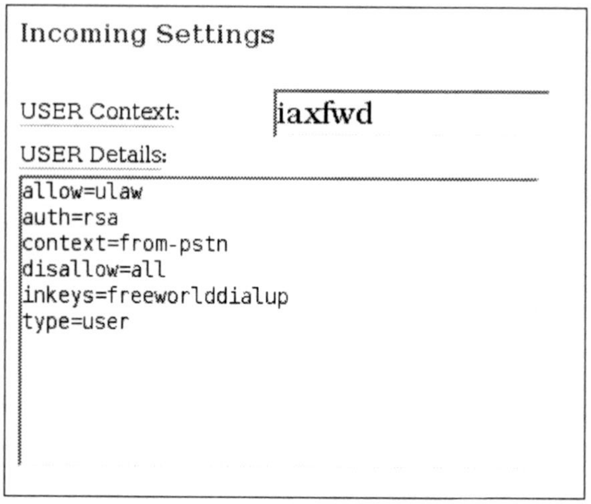

Incoming Settings

USER Context: iaxfwd

USER Details:

```
allow=ulaw
auth=rsa
context=from-pstn
disallow=all
inkeys=freeworlddialup
type=user
```

The **Register String** in the **Registration** screen is required for registering our device with Free World Dialup. The **myfwdnumber** and **mysecret** should be replaced with our Free World Dialup telephone number and password respectively.

Registration

Register String:

myfwdnumber:mysecret@iax2.fwdnet.net

We now need to configure a route so that calls that are destined for this trunk will be routed through it. This is done by clicking on the **Outbound Routes** link, on the left-hand side menu and filling in the form shown as follows:

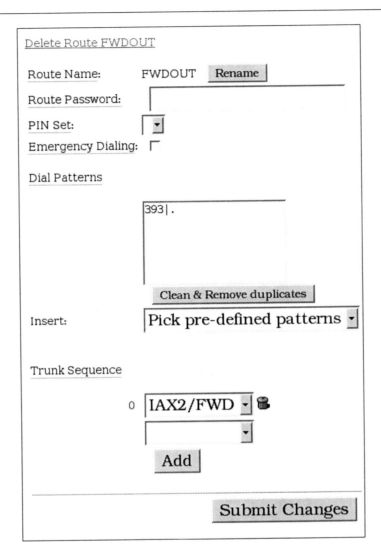

The screenshot displays the following options:

- **Route Name**: The route name is a unique name for the route.
- **Route Password**: The route password can be used to protect this route from being accessed without a password.
- **PIN Set**: A pin number can be used for security, instead of a password, if set here.
- **Emergency Dialing**: This should be checked if the route will be used for emergency calls as it will replace the CID with the CID provided by the device.

- **Dialplan Patterns**: We will have a closer look at dialplan patterns later, but in this case it means that all calls that are initiated to numbers beginning with **393** will go through this route. The **Insert** field, however, has some standard patterns.

- **Trunk Sequence**: The order in which the trunks will be used, if they match the given dialplan pattern. In this case, we have only one. However, if we had more, when the FWD trunk met its limit of four calls we would then start using the next trunk listed.

Assuming we have configured everything correctly, we should now be able to dial **393612**, which will read out the time to us. If you are feeling exceptionally brave, we can dial **393613**, which is a useful echo-tester. It will just bounce back to us everything we say to it, which is good for testing that we have everything working, from the audio settings of our phone to the connection with Free World Dialup. We can then try **393514,** which is FWD's *Coffee Lounge*, or **39355555**, which calls a random volunteer, so we can actually speak to a live person! It can be quite fun calling these first two numbers and chatting away with the other Free World Dialup users.

Setting Up a PSTN Trunk

If we have purchased an X100P card, Digium TDM400 card, or an Asterisk Developer Kit (which includes a TDM400 card), then we are ready to configure a trunk to talk to the PSTN. We will need to log in directly to the server, or through an SSH client.

Once we have logged into the system, run the `genzaptelconf` script by typing `genzaptelconf` on the command line. This will automatically configure our card for us. If it completes successfully, we should see a text output like this:

```
[root@asterisk1 ~]# genzaptelconf

STARTING FOP SERVER
FOP Server Started
Chan   Extension Context        Language    MusicOnHold
pseudo           from-pstn      en
  1              from-pstn      en
```

If you we see the pseudo line, then the system did not properly detect our card. If we see one or more channels, then our card has been properly detected and configured.

Inbound Routing

Inbound routing takes incoming calls and routes them to their destination. It is also known as DID or Direct Inward Dialing. Inbound routing is based on the phone number the calling party dialled to determine the caller's destination. Every setup that will accept incoming calls will have at least one incoming route. In larger setups, individual users or departments may get their own DID numbers.

The most basic configuration of an inbound route is to simply specify the inbound phone number and select a destination. However, FreePBX allows for some additional configuration options. By clicking on the **Inbound Route** link on the left-hand side FreePBX menu, we reach this section:

- **DID Number**: This specifies the phone number the calling party dialled in order to reach you.

- **Caller-ID Number**: This setting allows us to route calls based on the phone number the calling party was using when they placed the call to you. The best example of using this setting is to create the 'ex-girlfriend' mode to put certain people into a special extension or menu. This is also good for routing special VIP clients to a priority queue for faster support.

- **Zaptel Channel**: If we don't want to match on the DIDs above we can match on the specific Zaptel channel used.

```
Add Incoming Route
...............................................................................

DID Number:          [                    ]

Caller ID Number:    [                    ]


OR

Zaptel Channel:      [                    ]
```

- **Fax Extension**: We can configure faxes to go to any extension or to the system fax extension as configured in the **General Settings** section later in this chapter.

- **Fax Email**: If the email address for sending faxes is blank, the email address set in the **General Settings** is used. In general, it's advisable to leave this entire section blank and use the general settings, for simplicity.

- **Fax Detection Type**: This detects faxes by checking for faxes on incoming calls.

- **Pause after answer**: If we are using fax detection, then we will need to set this option to the number of seconds to wait after answering a call to determine if there are fax tones present.

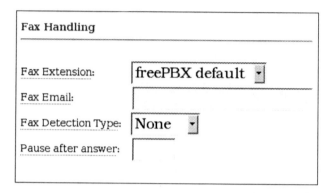

- **Privacy Manager**: When the privacy manager is turned on and no caller-id is detected on the line, the system will prompt the caller for their 10-digit phone number before continuing.

- **Alert Info**: This is used to modify the ring used with SIP devices.

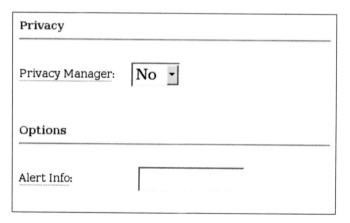

- **Set Destination**: The final step in configuring the incoming route is setting the destination. The destination for any inbound call can be a digital receptionist, extension, voicemail, ring group, queue, custom application, time condition, or any other currently available destination.

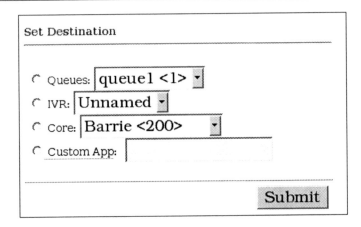

Outbound Routing

One of the tricky concepts while configuring TrixBox is learning how to create good outbound routing rules. A primary usage of outbound routing rules that has been common for many years is least-cost routing. With traditional PBX systems, we might have used least-cost routing to pick one provider for local calls, another for in-state calls, and yet another for out-of-state calls. In some cases, this is still a valid usage of outbound routing rules. With a modern PBX such as Asterisk, there are many reasons to set up different outbound rules:

- Send **999/911/611** calls to an analog line to ensure that emergency calls go out through the analog lines.
- Use a different provider for international calls for cost savings. We can use VoIP for our international calls and go through an ITSP for substantial cost savings.
- Send toll-free calls through a specific provider.
- Use different rules if users dial **9** first, for example to use **9** for an outside line.

By default, TrixBox sets up a simple calling plan that pushes any call starting with **9** through a Zaptel trunk. If we are only setting up VoIP trunks, we will have to modify the default rule. An outbound routing rule is made up of several components:

- **Route Name**
- **Route Password** (prompts users for passwords; useful for blocking access to premium-rate numbers)
- **Dialplan patterns** (defines which calls go through this route)
- **Trunk sequence** (the order in which different trunks are assigned to this route)

Add Route

Route Name: [   ]

Route Password: [   ]

PIN Set: [▼]

Emergency Dialing: ☐

Dial Patterns

[   ]

[Clean & Remove duplicates]

Insert: [Pick pre-defined patterns ▼]

Trunk Sequence

[▼]

[Add]

[Submit Changes]

Dialplan Patterns

We should take care to create valid dialplans so as to ensure that our calls are handled via the appropriate trunks.

Many people get confused about dialplan pattern construction; but it doesn't have to be that difficult. The following table lists the special dialplan pattern characters and their significance:

Special Dialplan Pattern Characters	Significance
X	Matches any digit from 0-9
Z	Matches any digit from 1-9
N	Matches any digit from 2-9
[1237-9]	Matches any digit or letter in the brackets (in this example, 1,2,3,7,8,9)
.	Wildcard; matches one or more characters
|	Separates dialing prefix from number
+	Adds preceding digits to number

Now, **9|.** will take the dialed string **917145551212**, match the number because it begins with **9**, separate it from the phone number, and send out the remaining digits to the ZAP/g0 trunk.

Let us look at two other common uses for a dialplan pattern: VoIP trunks that require full area-code dialing, and passing extensions to another server. Some ITSP's don't match our account with the local area code, especially those that only provide outbound dialing. In this case, we will need to add a **1** plus an area code to any number that was dialled with only seven digits. To accomplish this, let's assume we need to add **1714** to local numbers. For this, we would use the `1714+NXXXXXX` pattern.

This would result in any seven digit number having **1714** added to it before it was sent out through the trunk.

In a large implementation, we may have groups of extensions located at different physical locations connected via trunk lines.

Suppose, location A has extensions **300** to **399** and location B has extensions **400** to **499**. At location A, our dialplan pattern would be **[4]XX**, which matches the number **4** with any two additional digits. At location B, our dialplan pattern would be **[3]xx**, which matches the number **3** with any two additional digits.

To help us with the basic dialplan pattern creation, the FreePBX has a pull-down menu of common patterns that we can use for basic setups.

Trunk Sequence

The final phase of creating the dialplan is setting the trunk sequence. Not all dialplans have multiple trunks available for use, such as the remote extensions example. In other cases, such as long-distance dialing, our preferred carrier would be first, followed by a backup provider in case we max out the available channels, or if the system was unable to contact the primary provider. We can choose our trunk sequence from the drop-down menu as seen in the preceding screenshot.

Digital Receptionist

Asterisk's digital receptionist feature is the key to making a small company's phone system portray an image of professionalism. Smaller PBX systems usually require expensive upgrades to get IVR functionality. The FreePBX interface makes creating the menu system fairly simple.

Let's take a look at **a typical voice** menu system for a small company:

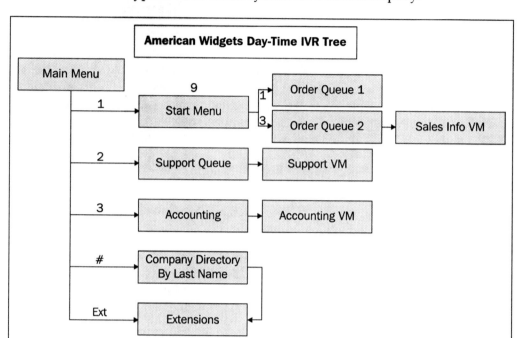

From the diagram, we can see how the main menu is delivered to the caller giving the caller several options to choose from. Based on the user's selection, he or she may be passed off to another menu, or directed to a queue or to the company directory.

Before creating an IVR menu, we will need to first create all the recordings we are going to use. Once we have our flowchart ready, we should next create the scripts for each of the voice prompts we will need. When we are ready, we need to go to the **System Recordings** module to record our prompts.

In the **System Recordings** screen, we can upload a .wav file or dial *77 to record a message. When we dial *77, we will only have a second or two before hearing a short tone that tells us to begin speaking. When finished, simply hang up. We can then dial *99 to verify that the file recorded properly. For our example layout, a script would be something like this:"*Thank you for calling American Widgets. If you know your party's extension, you can dial it at any time. For a company directory, press the pound key; for Sales press 1; for Support press 2; for Accounting, press 3. Please visit our website at www. superwidgets.com.*"

System Recordings

Add Recording

Step 1: Record or upload

If you wish to make and verify recordings from your phone, please enter your extension number here:

[   ] Go

Alternatively, upload a recording in .wav format:

[   ] Browse... Upload

Step 2: Name

Name this Recording: [   ]

Click "SAVE" when you are satisfied with your recording Save

It is recommend that we paste the script of the item into the description field and give it a descriptive name. We can do this by clicking on the name of the recording on the top-right corner, which should take us to a screen like this:

System Recordings

Add Recording

upload

Edit Recording

Remove Recording *(Note, does not delete file from computer)*

Change Name | upload

Descriptive Name | No long description available

Save

Once we have our recordings done, the next step is to begin to create our IVR menu.

The digital receptionist is used to create the IVR menus that the caller will hear when dialing into the system. The screenshot overleaf displays the settings screen for the IVR menu. We get to this screen by clicking on the **Digital Receptionist** link in the FreePBX menu. The first section of the screenshot sets the basic settings for each menu set including the ability for callers to access the company directory, the ability to directly dial extensions, and which system recordings to use as an announcement.

Digital Receptionist

Edit Menu Unnamed

Delete Digital Receptionist Unnamed

Change Name   Unnamed

Timeout   10

Enable Directory   ☑

Directory Context   ▢

Enable Direct Dial   ☑

Announcement   None ▾

Increase Options	Save	Decrease Options

     ○ IVR: Unnamed ▾
     ○ Custom App:

     ○ IVR: Unnamed ▾
     ○ Custom App:

     ○ IVR: Unnamed ▾
     ○ Custom App:

Increase Options	Save	Decrease Options

As we can see from the settings screen, there are a lot of options for each key that can be pressed. Some of these options may not appear on your system until you have configured them. The system is aware of your configuration options in other sections and displays those in this screen. The options that we can see on the screen are:

- **IVR**: This is used to branch to a sub-menu.
  - **Applications**: This is used to branch to custom applications we might have defined earlier in our dialplans.
  - **Conferences**: This is used to go directly to a pre-defined conference room.

- ○ **Core**: This is for selecting an extension or voicemail box.
- ○ **Ring Groups**: This is used to send callers to a pre-defined ring group.
- ○ **Queues**: This is used to send callers to a pre-defined call queue.
- ○ **DISA**: If we have a DISA (Direct Inward System Access) set configured, this will send callers to this application. We will learn more about DISA in Chapter 8.
- **Custom App**: If we have custom applications defined in our dialplan, we can use this selection to send callers into that context.

Ring Groups

Ring groups and **hunt** are among the more popular of the advanced features within TrixBox. With ring groups, we define a set of extensions that will perform a specified ring behavior.

Looking back at our example flow chart, if we wanted the phones of several people to ring whenever a caller hit **2** for support, we could create a support ring group. The most common **ring strategy** is the **ringall** setting. With the **ringall** setting, all the extensions in the extension list will ring at the same time. If we want an external phone such as a cell phone to ring, we will need to add the phone number to the list and put a pound sign at the end. If we put something into the **CID name prefix**, then it will prefix this to the caller's caller-id information allowing us to know on which ring group it came in. If we are calling out to an outside number, we may need to experiment with the ring time to prevent the call to the external phone number from being picked up by its own voicemail or answering machine.

Another of the ring strategies is the **hunt** method. With the **hunt** setting, the system takes turns calling each extension. While it allows a basic hierarchy of responsibility and keeps every phone from ringing at the same time, it can also keep a caller waiting longer to have their call answered.

The final ring strategy is actually a good means of accomplishing a "follow-me" setup, which is a highly requested feature. By using the **memoryhunt** setting, the system will ring the first extension in the list, then ring the first and second extension, then the first, second, and third, and so on.

Add Ring Group

Add Ring Group

group number: `1`

group description: `[               ]`

ring strategy: `ringall ▼`

extension list: `[         ▲▼]`

`Clean & Remove duplicates`

CID name prefix: `[       ]`

ring time (max 60 sec): `20`

announcement: `None ▼`

Alert Info: `[               ]`

Destination if no answer:

○ Core: `Kerry Garrison <200> ▼`

○ IVR: `Unnamed ▼`

○ Custom App: `[               ]`

`Submit Changes`

Queues

When call queues came out in older PBX systems, it had a dramatic difference on how calls were handled. Instead of users calling in and getting a busy signal if no operators were available, callers were now put into a holding room with music on-hold and even product information or support tips. Some of the most advanced systems would even tell us our place in the queue and an estimated hold time. Believe it or not, this Fortune-500 type of feature is built into the TrixBox installation. Queues also contain most of the settings of all the available features allowing us a tremendous amount of flexibility. The following list explains each of the available settings:

- **queue number**: Each queue must be assigned a unique number, just like extensions and ring groups. The queue number is also used for agents to log in and out of the queue. To log in, a user dials the queue number plus * (e.g. **123***) and to log out, the user needs to dial the queue number plus ** (e.g. **123****).

- **queue name**: Each queue can be assigned a name that is used for display purposes only.

- **queue password**: The queue password is an optional setting that we can use to require the agents to use a password to log into the queue.

- **CID name prefix**: If the CID name prefix is set, then it will prefix the caller's caller-id with the text in this field.

- **static agents**: If some extensions are always supposed to be in a particular queue, then those extensions can be listed as static agents. If we do not have any static agents, then our users will have to log into the queue in order for the system to send callers to them.

Apart from these settings, there are some more **Queue Options** as shown in the following screenshot:

Queue Options	
Agent Announcement:	None
Hold Music Category:	Default
max wait time:	Unlimited
max callers:	0
join empty:	Yes
leave when empty:	No
ring strategy:	ringall
agent timeout:	15 seconds
retry:	5 seconds
wrap-up-time:	0 seconds
call recording:	No

The following list explains the settings for these options:

- **Agent Announcement**: If we have recorded a custom message, this can be played to the agent prior to the call being transferred. This can be something like *"Transfering call from the support queue"*. To add announcements, we use the **System Recordings** menu.

- **Hold Music Category**: We can define different groups of music on-hold recordings in the **On-Hold Music** system. The next section covers on-hold music in more detail and how we can add more categories. By using different groups, we can do things like having sales and product information played in the sales queue and support tips played in the support queue.

- **max wait time**: This setting allows us to adjust the maximum amount of time a caller can wait in the queue before being transferred as a no-answer.

- **max callers**: We can set the maximum number of callers that can be in a queue at any time. This can be used to prevent all our available lines from being taken up by users lined up in the queue.

- **join empty**: If we want callers to be able to join a queue that has no active agents, then set this to **yes**; otherwise, set this to **no**.

- **leave when empty**: If this setting is set to **yes**, then any caller who is currently in the queue will automatically be dropped into the failover condition when the last agent leaves the queue.

- **ring strategy**: Similar to the ring group strategy settings, we can use different ring settings to determine the call flow of the queue. The ring strategy supports multiple settings including **ringall**, **round robin**, **least recent**, **fewest calls**, **random**, and **round robin with memory**.

- **agent timeout**: This sets the amount of time an agent's extension can ring before the system considers it a timeout.

- **retry**: This specifies the number of seconds to wait before retrying all the agents again.

- **wrap-up time**: After an agent finishes a call, this setting adjusts the amount of time to wait before sending another call to this agent. This will need to be adjusted to match the workflow of the agents.

- **call recording**: This setting toggles whether or not all the calls placed through the queue will be recorded. We can also configure **Caller Announcements** in the following screenshot:

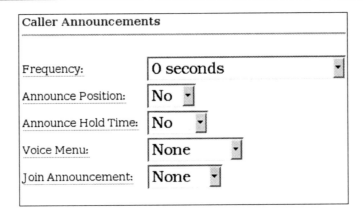

- **Frequency**: This setting adjusts the frequency to announce the caller's queue position.

- **Announce Position**: This setting toggles whether or not to announce the caller's position in the queue.

- **Announce Hold Time**: This setting toggles whether or not to announce the estimate hold time.

- **Voice Menu**: This setting allows us to specify a digital receptionist menu that we can present to the user after announcing the caller's position.

- **Join Announcement**: If we have recorded a message, we can use this setting to play a custom message to the caller before sending them into the queue.

- **Fail Over Destination**: Just like ring groups, we can determine where a call should go if the caller gets bumped from the queue. This can be a digital receptionist menu, an extension, a voicemail box, a ring group, another queue, or a custom app. An example of this would be failing over to a voicemail box during night hours when nobody is available to answer a call.

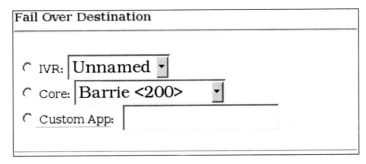

Music On-Hold

As part of our queues, we could choose which category of on-hold music to use. We are limited to one by default, but we can add our own by clicking on the **On-Hold Music** link on the left-hand side of the FreePBX menu.

This is a simple management tool for uploading and organizing our music on-hold files. We can also create categories for grouping our files into sets that can be used in different sections of the system.

The following screenshot shows the **Default** category. We can select other categories by clicking the name of that category on the top right.

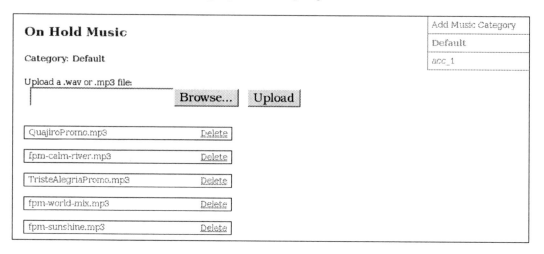

If we click on the **Add Music Category** link, we will see the following screen:

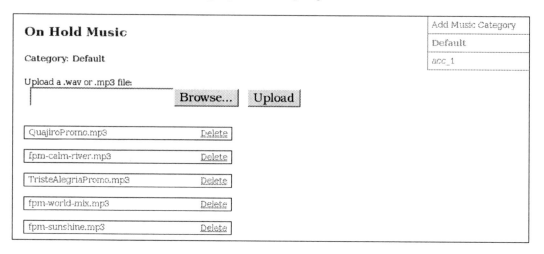

Here we can input a new category by simply entering its name and clicking **Submit Changes**.

General Settings

The **General Settings** section is located on the left-hand side of the FreePBX menu and has a few settings that don't fit anywhere else. The options that can be set from here are briefly explained in the following sections.

Dialing Options

Asterisk Dial command options can be set to any combination of the following:

- **t**: This allows the user receiving the call to transfer it. Transfers are initiated by pushing the # key on the user's phone.
- **T**: This allows the user placing the call to transfer it.
- **r**: This plays a ringing tone to the user calling in.
- **w**: This allows the user receiving the call to initiate call recording. Call recordings are initiated by pressing ***1**.
- **W**: This allows the user placing the call to initiate call recording.

Dialing Options	
Asterisk Dial command options:	tr
Asterisk Outbound Dial command options:	r

Voicemail

The following settings can be performed for voicemail from General Settings:

- The number of seconds to wait before going to voicemails is a good default at **15**, but can be modified if necessary.
- **Extension prefix for dialing direct to voicemail** should be left as it is. If it is changed, then the digits ***98** that we dial to reach our voicemail in this book will have to be amended.
- **Direct dial to voicemail message type** selects the pre-defined message to be played to users who dial voicemail.
- Gain should be added if the voicemail recording is too quiet when played back.

Voicemail

Number of seconds to ring phones before sending callers to voicemail: `15`

Extension prefix for dialing direct to voicemail: `*`

Direct Dial to Voicemail message type: `Default ▼`

Use gain when recording the voicemail message (optional): [_____]

Company Directory

The company directory can be configured to find users by **last name** or by **first name**. By ticking the **Play extension number to caller before transferring call** box, the caller can hear the recipient's number before being put straight through.

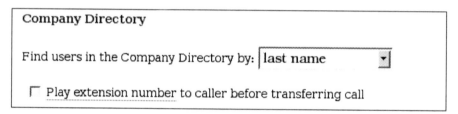

Company Directory

Find users in the Company Directory by: `last name ▼`

☐ Play extension number to caller before transferring call

Fax Settings

Faxes can be sent to any extension number by selecting an appropriate destination in the first drop-down menu (please be sure the extension has a fax attached). Faxes can also be emailed to an email address and the **From** header on the email can be configured to something such as **faxmachine@company.com**.

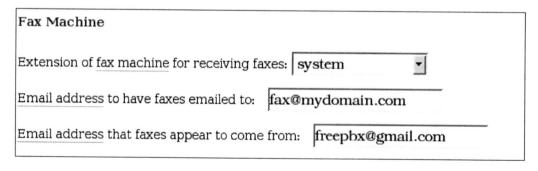

Fax Machine

Extension of fax machine for receiving faxes: `system ▼`

Email address to have faxes emailed to: `fax@mydomain.com`

Email address that faxes appear to come from: `freepbx@gmail.com`

International Settings

Here we should be sure to select the correct country/region.

Security Settings

If we do not want people to call into our PBX using the SIP VoIP protocol, then we should leave this at **no**. Changing to **yes** will let people call SIP extensions on our PBX without first logging in with a user name and password.

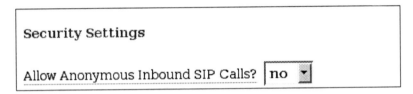

Summary

In this chapter, we have covered the configuration of our TrixBox system in order to get some of the common telephony functions set up. We can set up extensions, trunks, ring groups, queues, and even full-featured IVR systems! In the following chapters, we will cover how many of the different functions work as well as troubleshooting for those situations where things don't always go smoothly.

7
Standard PBX Features

As with any commercial PBX system, Asterisk has a slew of advanced features that are activated by key commands, also known as **vertical activation codes**.

Standard Features

The following sections briefly explain the current list of available features that are standard in TrixBox. While the codes listed are the default setting, they can be modified using the FreePBX **Features** module. These codes are all used by dialing the number on a phone that is logged into the system by SIP/IAX, or by connecting a traditional phone to a card installed in the system.

Call Forwarding

The call forwarding functions have a lot of capabilities. While some variations don't get much usage, a popular one is the *Call Forwarding on No Answer*. With this, we could create a multi-tier calling system like those found on high-end systems. If our regular phone doesn't answer, then it could forward the call to a ring group containing alternative numbers such as cell phone numbers and residence numbers.

Function	Code
Call Forward All Activate	*72
Call Forward All Deactivate	*73
Call Forward All Prompting Deactivate	*74
Call Forward Busy Activate	*90
Call Forward Busy Deactivate	*91
Call Forward Busy Prompting Deactivate	*92
Call Forward No Answer/Unavailable Activate	*52
Call Forward No Answer/Unavailable Deactivate	*53

Call Waiting

Call waiting, as most people know, is the beep that we hear when a second call comes in allowing us to flash-hook our phone to switch lines. With Asterisk, this feature enables multiple calls to come through our phone if we have a phone that supports multiple call appearances. By default, call waiting is disabled on every extension. This default behavior can be changed by editing the /etc/amportal.conf file and setting **ENABLECW** to **yes**.

Function	Code
Call Waiting: Activate	*70
Call Waiting: Deactivate	*71

Core

It is not always convenient to continually dial into our system to see how our menus are processed. Using this feature, we can simulate incoming calls to see how they will be handled.

Function	Code
Simulate Incoming Call	7777
Simulate Incoming FAX Call	666

Do-Not-Disturb

The Do-Not-Disturb (DND) feature is great for phones that do not have a DND function on the phone itself. This will simply reroute all inbound calls directly to our voicemail.

Function	Code
DND Activate	*78
DND Deactivate	*79

Info Services

This feature contains a few tools to make sure our system is working properly.

Function	Code
Call Trace	*69
Directory	#
Echo Test	*43
Speak our Extension Number	*65
Speaking Clock	*60

Recordings

When using the Recording module, these functions help us to record and play back the recordings we are making.

Function	Code
Check Recording	*77
Save Recording	*99

Device Control

When working with ad hoc devices, the user logon/logoff functions allow us to take control of the device. The ZapBarge function will allow us to listen, once calls are placed over Zap channels.

Function	Code
User Logoff	*12
User Logon	*11
ZapBarge	888

Active-Call Codes

During a phone call, there are a number of functions that are available to us. While some functions may be available on our actual phone device, others are only available through key commands:

Function	Code
Enter call transfer mode	#
Park current call	#70
Begin recording call	*1
End recording call	*2
Transfer directly to dialled extension's voicemail box	*+Extension

System-Wide Speed Dialling

The current versions of TrixBox now contain a system-wide speed dialing system. This system uses extension from 300 to 399. So we need to keep this in mind when designing our extension layout. If we need to use extensions in the 3xx range, we will need to disable or renumber the speed dial system in `extensions_custom.conf`.

The following chart shows the commands for the speed dial system:

Function	Action Code
Add a new speed dial to extension 300 to 399	3003xx+Phone Number
Speak the current speed dial setting	*3xx
Dial the specified speed dial number	3xx

Voicemail

TrixBox comes with the **Asterisk Mail Voicemail System**. Asterisk Mail is a very capable voicemail system. The voicemail system can be accessed by any internal phone, or when dialling into the automated attendant.

There are two entry points to the voicemail, "Dial Voicemail" and "My Voicemail". For Dial Voicemail, if we dial ***97** from an extension, it will bypass the standard login and ask for the password of the caller's extension. For My Voicemail, dialling ***98** will prompt the caller for their extension and then their password.

The voicemail main menu options are listed in the following chart:

Option	Code
Listen to (New) Messages	1
Change Folders	2
Mailbox Options	0
Help	*
Exit	#

The option "Listen to (New) Messages" has some sub-options that are listed in the following chart:

Option	Code
Repeat Message	5
Play Next Message	6
Delete Message	7
Forward to another user	8
Save Message	9
New Messages	0
Old Messages	1
Work Messages	2
Family Messages	3
Friends Messages	4
Help	*
Cancel/Exit to Main Menu	#

As seen from the table, if we wish to forward to another user, we need to press **8**. Further, we need to enter the appropriate extension number and press **#**. If we press **1**, it will prepend a message to a forwarded message. Pressing **2** will forward without prepending.

The Change folders option also has some sub-options that are listed in the following table:

Option	Code
New Messages	0
Old Messages	1
Work Messages	2
Family Messages	3
Friends Messages	4
Cancel/Exit to Main Menu	#

The "Mailbox options" in the Voicemail main menu also come with some options that are listed in the following chart:

Option	Code
Record our Un-Available Message	1
Record our Busy message	2
Record our Name	3
Change our Password	4
Cancel/Exit to Main Menu	#

Asterisk Recording Interface (ARI)

The ARI system is a web interface available from the main web interface. Using the ARI system, a user can enter their extension and voicemail password and have access to their new and old voicemail recordings, call recordings, and call history.

Using the ARI interface, a user can control several user settings such as:

- Default Language
- Change Password
- Sound file quality
- Incoming Call Recording Settings
- Outbound Call Recording Settings

The following two screenshots display the voicemail interface and the call monitor screen for any user, respectively:

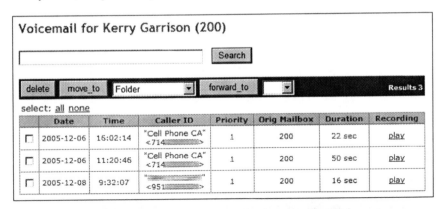

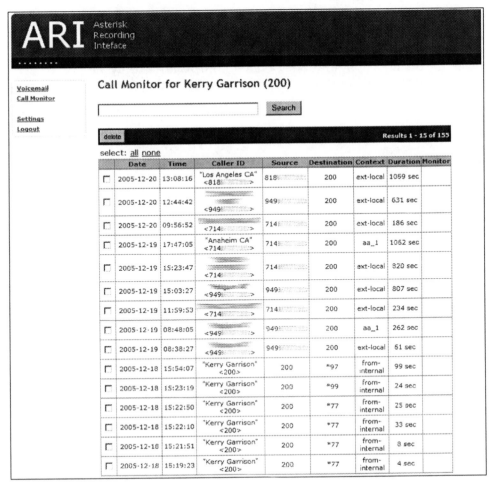

Flash Operator Panel

The **Flash Operator Panel** is an operator switchboard control panel that runs in a web browser as a Flash applet. The Flash Operator Panel constantly polls the Asterisk server to update the buttons on the screen. The layout is very configurable for different scenarios. It can also integrate with CRM software by popping up a web page when a specified button rings. In the Flash Operator Panel, we can see at a glance:

- Which extensions are busy, ringing, or available
- Who is talking and to whom (CID, context, priority)
- SIP and IAX registration status and reachability
- MeetMe room status (number of participants)
- Queue status (number of users waiting)
- Message Waiting Indicator and count
- Parked channels
- Logged-in Agents

However, the default configuration is a bit limiting as it will only support 38 extensions and 19 trunks, and does not have a configuration for MeetMe rooms.

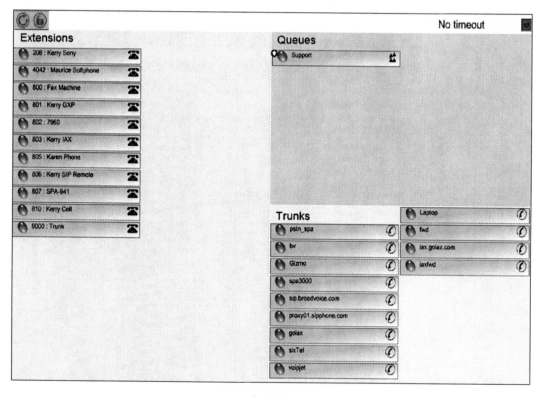

Using the Flash Operator Panel

When an extension or a trunk is in use, the green oval will turn to red as a visual indicator. As additional information becomes available, it is added to the button itself. A flashing oval indicates that the channel is currently ringing.

If there is activity on a button and we move the mouse over it, we will see additional information in the status bar. For each session, the first time we try to perform an action, we will be prompted for the security code; the default security code is **passw0rd**. The actions that we can perform from the Flash Operator Panel are:

- Hang-up a channel (double-click the colored dot on the button)
- Transfer a call via drag-and-drop (drag the phone icon on a button to another button)
- Originate calls via drag-and-drop (drag an available channel to another available channel)
- Barge in on a call via drag-and-drop (drag an available channel to a bridged channel)
- Set the caller-id when transferring or originating a call
- Automatically pop up web page with customer details
- Click-to-Dial from a web page
- Mute/unmute MeetMe participants

Wakeup Calls

The **Wakeup Call** system is a fairly simple script that was written in PHP. To access the Wakeup Call function, we need to dial ***62** from a device. The system will ask us for the time we would like to have our wakeup call. At the specified time, the system will ring our extension and play back the current music on-hold files.

This is a good example of an AGI script; to take a look at this or other scripts, we can look in the folder `/var/lib/asterisk/agi-bin/`.

Weather Report

Out of the box, TrixBox is configured to use ***61** to fetch a weather report for New York City. If we would like to customize this, it requires a small amount of work to look up the correct values and edit the required files. Following are the steps that we need to perform to customize this feature:

1. Use an FTP client or Internet Explorer to go to `ftp://weather.noaa.gov/data/forecasts/city/`.

2. Go into the appropriate folder for our state (example, ca for California).

3. Find the city closest to our location (example, `san_francisco.txt`).

4. Log in to our Asterisk server console.

5. Use the command `cd /var/lib/asterisk/agi-bin`.

6. Use the command `nano weather.agi`.

7. The two lines we need to edit are:
   ```
   my $custpath = "city/ny";
   my $filename = "new_york.txt";
   ```

8. Using our example, we will edit them as follows:
   ```
   my $custpath = "city/ca";
   my $filename = "san_francisco.txt";
   ```

9. Use *Ctrl+x* to exit the editor and hit *Y* to save changes.

Summary

This chapter introduced us to the basic Asterisk features and common tools that are included with TrixBox. We should now be able to use all the built-in functions and the voicemail system. Although some features can be changed and modified, we should have all the information we need to run a standard system.

8
Advanced TrixBox Settings

In this chapter, we will have a look at some of the other features and considerations for our TrixBox deployment. We will cover conferencing, some advanced management options, and how to add tools. We will also cover adding other line types to our TrixBox system. By this point, we have enough to have a system up and running and to manage all our basic requirements. This chapter looks at extending those features to give us some extra features.

Firewall Settings

If we are going to use any remote extensions or ITSPs, sooner or later we will need to deal with firewall issues. Unfortunately, the SIP protocol is not very friendly with firewalls and Network Address Translation (NAT).

SIP as a protocol design makes sense, if every computer on the Internet has a unique IP address. However, in many cases, the computers sit behind a firewall that performs NAT of some kind and is the only device with a publicly accessible IP address. This makes it quite difficult to manage sessions between machines as it requires a number of ports to be open to the machines involved in the connection. What this means is that we often have calling problems with NAT on our network, usually with a lack of audio or an inability to initiate calls.

To get around this, we will need to open some ports in our firewall to the TrixBox system. The following table lists the ports required for Asterisk to function efficiently:

Ports	Protocol	Description
4569	UDP	IAX2 Support
5060-5061	UDP	SIP Ports
10,000-20,000	UDP	SIP Support

The steps to open these ports on our firewall differ, depending on the particular device or software we use. However, it is generally referred to as **"Port Forwarding"** or something similar to this. For example, if we are using a SOHO router, these generally have a web interface with a section for forwarding ports.

NAT Considerations

When we have a device performing NAT between our TrixBox system and our providers, we can remedy this by making some changes to our configuration. We can manually change the configuration files from the web interface in order to make any changes for which we can find options. To reach this section, from the first page of the TrixBox web interface click the **System Administration** link as shown below:

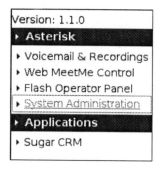

Next, we should see the **System Administration** screen where we click on **Config Edit**.

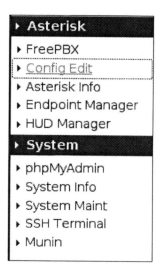

Here, we can see all the notable configuration files involved with our TrixBox system that we can change manually.

p h p c o n f i g f o r A s t e r i s k P B X				
/etc/asterisk	/var/www/html/panel	/etc	/tftpboot	Re-Read Configs

a2billing.conf
agents.conf
alarmreceiver.conf
applications.conf
asterisk.conf
cdr_mysql.conf
codecs.conf
dnsmgr.conf
dundi.conf
enum.conf
extconfig.conf
extensions.conf
extensions_additional.conf
extensions_custom.conf
extensions_hud.conf
extensions_trixbox.conf
features.conf

We want to modify the `sip_nat.conf` file, so click on it to show us the file:

Edit: sip_nat.conf

```
[general]
externip=55.66.77.88 ; Change to match our external IP address
localnet=192.168.1.0/255.255.255.0 ; Change to match our network settings
```

We want to add the following information as shown in the preceding screenshot:

```
[general]
externip=55.66.77.88 ; Change to match our external IP address
localnet=192.168.1.0/255.255.255.0; Change to match our network settings
```

The `externip` setting needs to be set to our public IP address. If we do not know what our public IP address is, use a browser and go to `http://whatismyip.com`. Be aware that if we do not have a static IP address and our ISP changes our IP address, then any remote user or ITSP connection will fail until we reset our `externip` setting and restart Asterisk. This is one of the reasons that having a static IP address is extremely beneficial, especially when using a VoIP system.

The second setting, `localnet`, tells Asterisk what IP range the server sits on. So, Asterisk knows how to listen correctly for requests. `localnet` should be set to whatever our internal IP range is on our local area network.

For any remote extensions, we will need to edit the extension and change the setting for NAT to **yes**. This tells Asterisk that the extension is not on the same network as the server.

However, once we get our system up and running, if we are only getting audio on one side of the conversation, it is almost always a problem with the NAT configuration.

Configuring Zaptel Cards

Usually, the hardware devices people use when experimenting with TrixBox are Zaptel cards such as the X100P or TDM400 cards. If we have one of these cards in our system, we will need to run the configuration script. To set up Zaptel cards, run the following setup script:

```
[root@asterisk1 ~]# genzaptelconf
STOPPING ASTERISK
Disconnected from Asterisk server
Asterisk Stopped
STOPPING FOP SERVER
FOP Server Stopped
Generating  '/etc/zaptel.conf'
Generating  '/etc/asterisk/zapata-auto.conf'
Unloading zaptel hardware drivers:
Unloading ztdummy:                                      [  OK  ]
. . . .
```

Some of the output has been truncated here for brevity, but once complete we will be back at the command prompt:

```
[root@asterisk1 ~]#
```

This script, as its name suggests, generates a file called `zaptel.conf` that can be found in the `/etc/` directory. We can view this file by running:

```
[root@asterisk1 ~]# cat /etc/zaptel.conf
```

In the case of a TDM400 card with four FXO modules, the file shows four configured modules that look like the following:

 # Span 1: WCTDM/0 "Wildcard TDM400P Board 1"
fxsks=1
fxsks=2
fxsks=3
fxsks=4

Configuring T1/E1 Cards

The automatic configuration script does not work with Digium digital line cards. These will need to be configured manually. Two files will need to be edited for Asterisk to be able to use these cards. Here, we will see how to configure a Digium TE110P card.

From the Asterisk server, we will need to edit or create a file called `zaptel.conf`.

```
[root@asterisk1 ~]# nano /etc/zaptel.conf
```

Now we need to type in the following information:

```
# TE110P T1 Card / Typical US Settings
span=1,1,0,esf,b8zs
bchan=1-23
dchan=24
```

Hit *Ctrl+O* to save our changes and *Ctrl+X* to exit.

This information has now defined the card and how it communicates with the outside world as well as its capacities.

Next, we need to define the channels and how they function within Asterisk.

```
[root@asterisk1 ~]# nano /etc/asterisk/zapata.con
```

Type in the following information:

```
[channels]
switchtype=national
context=from-pstn
```

```
signalling=pri_cpe
group=1
channel => 1-23
language=en
context=from-pstn
signalling=fxs_ks
```

This defines the signalling, the group number, and what channels belong to that group. A complete explanation of these settings is outside of the scope of this book. In this example, the group is set to 1, which contains all the available channels. However, during trunk configuration, this will be important to remember.

Overhead Paging

A common request of larger companies is the ability to do overhead paging. Overhead paging is a system such as those used in airports, supermarkets, and train stations to make announcements. On our TrixBox system this is done by setting up an extension that can be called in order to make announcements.

We require a sound card in the TrixBox server. There are two steps to enable paging. Firstly, add the paging lines to the dialplan, and secondly, enable the sound card output within Linux.

To do the configurations, we need to go back to the **Config Edit** page that we accessed earlier. This time we are interested in the `extensions_custom.conf` file.

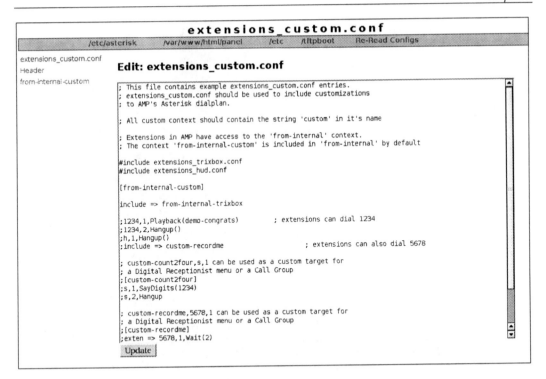

Here we are interested in the **[from-internal-custom]** section as shown in the screenshot. We want to add the following lines here:

```
exten => *52,1,Dial(console/dsp)
exten => *52,2,Hangup()
```

To enable the sound card, we need to run the `alsamixer` program.

```
[root@asterisk1 ~]# alsamixer
```

We can access the paging system by dialling ***52** and then start talking. We can adjust the volume by running the `alsamixer` program as shown overleaf to get our desired volume level. The mixer will adjust the sound volume in real time allowing us to adjust the volume while talking, so we can be sure the volume is set correctly. Once we run `alsamixer`, we need to un-mute the **Master** volume and **PCM** controls by using the *M* key on the keyboard and for adjusting the volume we can use the up and down arrows on the keyboard.

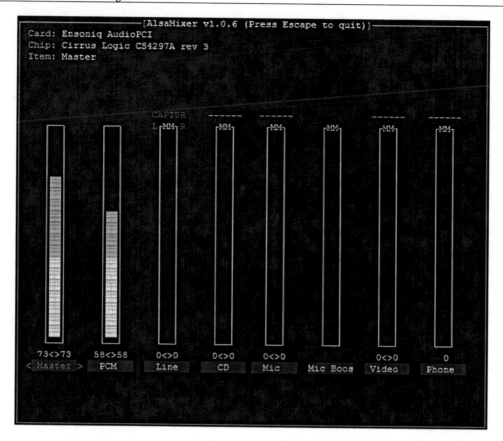

Caller-ID Blocking

If we are using PSTN circuits and want to be able to block caller-id, this simple script can be used to send the ***67** code to the phone line:

```
exten => *67,1,Dial(ZAP/1/*67 )
exten => *67,2,Wait(3)
exten => *67,3,SoftHangup(ZAP/1)
exten => *67,5,DISA(no-password|from-internal)
```

Caller-ID Blocking

*67 is the code used in the US to prevent the caller-id being displayed. In countries other than the US, this might differ. For example, in the UK we should dial the numbers **141**. We should check that our providers offer this option and that we have the correct code.

If we read through the code, we can see that the script dials ***67** through the first available PSTN line, performs a soft hang-up, which doesn't actually release the line, and then returns back a dial tone that will enable us to dial out to the number we want to call.

Making Free Directory-Assistance Calls

Several new companies have cropped up to allow free directory-assistance calls. These are usually prefaced by a short advertisement that we have to listen to. However, it is difficult to make all our employees remember to dial some other phone number for directory assistance. The easier way is to make Asterisk and FreePBX to route calls placed to **411** or **5551212** to one of these free services.

Directory Assistance

These numbers are used for directory assistance in the US. These may again differ depending on our telecommunications provider or country. For example, in the UK these are the 118 numbers, such as **118118** or **118247**.

From FreePBX main screen, click **Setup | Trunks | Add Custom Trunk**.

We would then configure it as shown in the screenshot overleaf for setting up the ability to call **411-METRO**.

Add CUSTOM Trunk

General Settings

Outbound Caller ID:

Maximum channels:

Outgoing Dial Rules

Dial Rules:

[Clean & Remove duplicates]

Dial rules wizards: (pick one)   ▼

Outbound Dial Prefix:

Outgoing Settings

Custom Dial String: IAX2/fwd/*18004116387

[Submit Changes]

Note that we need to specify the technology (SIP, IAX2, ZAP), the Trunk name (FWD), and the phone number to dial. In the case of FWD, we need to add * before the toll-free number. With other providers, we can omit the *.

Next, we go to the **Outbound Routes** module. Here, we will need to create a new route. We should call it something descriptive like `DirectoryAssist`. In the **Dialplan Patterns**, we need to add any pattern a user might dial to reach a normal directory assistance system:

```
411
5551212
1NXX5551212
NXX5551212
```

We now need to ensure our route is configured to use this new custom trunk. This is done by clicking on **Outbound Routing** then clicking on our **FWDOUT** trunk and adding the custom trunk list as shown in the screenshot below:

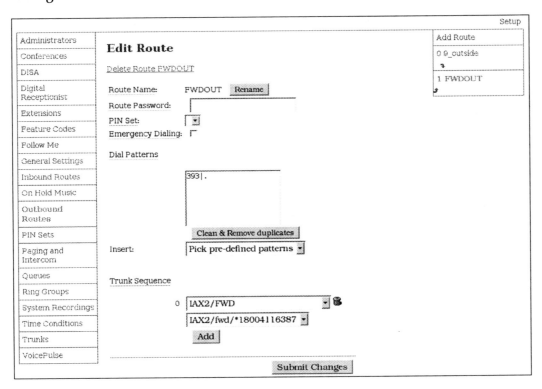

Predictive Diallers

Some companies will use dialling systems to make sure their agents are taking as many phone calls as possible. These systems will predict when the next agent will be available to take a call and then place an outbound call in anticipation of the agent freeing up on time. This ensures a constant flow of calls to the agents. There are currently several dialler options available in both open-source and commercial-product offerings.

In open-source there is ViciDial (`http://astguiclient.sourceforge.net/vicidial.html`) and GnuDialer (`http://www.gnudialer.org`), and in commercial-product offerings we have SineDialer (`http://sineapps.com`).

Advanced Reporting Tools

In a call center environment, reporting on agent and queue activity is extremely important. Although TrixBox has some basic call reports, they are often inadequate for larger companies. The first company to deliver an advanced reporting tool is QueMetrics (http://www.quemetrics.com). It has even created a simplified script to get a demo version installed on TrixBox in just a few minutes!

Outlook Integration

A popular feature of newer phone systems is the ability to dial directly from Microsoft Outlook's **Contact** list. This is most often accomplished with a TAPI interface such as the open-source ASTAPI plug-in (http://www.voip-info.org/wiki/view/Asterisk+TAPI). This will provide the most basic calling ability from Outlook, but doesn't get a lot of updates and some people report having issues with it.

TAPI

TAPI stands for Telephone Application Programming Interface and is simply a method for programmers to control telephones and telephone systems from a PC.

A newer product that has recently come out is 'Snap' (http://www.snapanumber.com), which takes dialling to a whole new level. Not only does Snap integrate with Outlook, but also it interfaces directly with our phone or SoftPhone to provide a complete call management and information system. Following is a very short list of the many features included in Snap:

- Call log
- Dial directly from call log
- Searchable
- Easily drag and drop phone numbers into Snap
- Enhanced caller-id when dialling
- For Outlook users, searches contacts for the proper caller-id name
- Hides in the system tray and does not bother us with annoying pop-ups or other nuisances
- Redials recently used phone numbers quickly
- Message-waiting indicator

- Includes a "Mini Snap bar", which efficiently uses our screen's real estate
- Tight integration for Outlook users; searches Outlook contacts, and opens them quickly
- Places recent calls in the system tray
- Supports automatic updates

DISA

Direct Inward System Access is used to provide access to "dial tone" from a call that originates outside the phone system. For a sales person that needs to place a sales call but doesn't want the caller-id of his/her cell phone to be displayed, the salesperson can call into the phone system, enter a code, and be dropped to a dial tone where the caller can dial out to any allowable phone number. Since the call was actually placed via the phone system, additional functionality like transferring the call to another extension is possible as the phone system is sitting between the caller and the person that was called.

[custom-disa]
exten => s,1,Answer
exten => s,2,DigitTimeout(5)
exten => s,3,ResponseTimeout(10)
exten => s,4,Authenticate(xxxx)
exten => s,5,DISA(no-password | from-internal)
changing xxxx for pin number

In our **Digital Receptionist** menu, add an option, preferably obscure like **8888** to point to **custom** and type the following line into the box:

```
custom-disa,s,1
```

You can now dial-in, get the attendant, dial **8888**, enter the pin number followed by #, and get an internal dial tone.

Feature Codes

The **Applications** module allows us to re-assign shortcut keys to commonly used applications such as access to the voicemail system and call-waiting settings. This is a frequently updated module as more feature codes are added on a regular basis.

Follow-Me

The **Follow-Me** function is a recent addition that allows multiple extensions to be assigned to a single person. Under the hood, this module actually creates a personal ring group for the selected extension as well as allows us to play an announcement to the callers letting them know that the system is trying to locate the person called.

Misc Destinations

This module allows us to create destinations that appear in different areas like IVR programming and fail-over destinations. The destination can be either a number that is dialled such as a cell phone number or it can be any of the scripts listed in the feature codes. For example, we may want a simple way of getting into voicemail remotely. We can create a destination called **voicemail-entry** and have it directed to the **Dial Voicemail** script. When creating our IVR menu, we can specify that dialling **9898** would point to **Misc Destination**: **voicemail-entry** putting us directly into the voicemail system.

Paging and Intercom

Although paging is a highly requested feature, it is actually fairly difficult to implement as there isn't really any standard that is implemented between phone manufacturers. The current implementation of paging and intercom should work with some Grandstream and SNOM phones, and hopefully will work with Linksys and Polycom phones shortly.

Time Conditions

The new **Time Conditions** module finally provides a method of creating multiple time-based menu options. The most common use of this is to automatically switch between settings used during normal business hours and settings that are used after business hours.

After giving our time condition a name, we set when we want this condition to be active. The format for the time setting is **time range | days of the week | days of the month | months**. A typical day/night setup might look something like this:

```
8:00-17:00|mon-fri|*|*
```

Server time: 17:59:51 | Add Time Condition
| Day Menu

Time Condition: 1

Delete Time Condition 1

Edit Time Condition

Time Condition name: Day Menu

Time to match: 8:00-17:00|mon-fri|*|*

Destination if time matches:

- ◉ IVR: Main IVR ▾
- ○ Applications: ▾
- ○ Conferences: ▾
- ○ Core: Kerry Garrison <100> ▾
- ○ Ring Groups: ▾
- ○ Time Conditions: Day Menu ▾
- ○ Queues: ▾
- ○ DISA: ▾
- ○ Custom App:

Destination if time does not match:

- ◉ IVR: Night ▾
- ○ Applications: ▾
- ○ Conferences: ▾
- ○ Core: Kerry Garrison <100> ▾
- ○ Ring Groups: ▾
- ○ Time Conditions: Day Menu ▾
- ○ Queues: ▾
- ○ DISA: ▾
- ○ Custom App:

Submit Changes

Installing WebMin

WebMin has been described as the Swiss Army Knife for Linux servers. Using WebMin, we can easily manage some of the more difficult Linux settings without having to mess with Linux config files.

To install WebMin, we need to find out which is the most current version. We can do this by visiting its website at http://www.webmin.com/. At the time of writing, the most current version was 1.250. This is important when it comes to getting the correct file.

To fetch and install the 1.250 version, use the following commands:

```
[root@asterisk1 ~]# cd /root

[root@asterisk1 ~]# mkdir webmin

[root@asterisk1 ~]# cd webmin

[root@asterisk1 webmin]# wget http://internap.dl.sourceforge.net/
sourceforge/webadmin/webmin-1.250-1.noarch.rpm

--22:47:25--  http://internap.dl.sourceforge.net/sourceforge/webadmin/
webmin-1.250-1.noarch.rpm

          => `webmin-1.250-1.noarch.rpm'
Resolving internap.dl.sourceforge.net... 64.74.207.43

Connecting to internap.dl.sourceforge.net|64.74.207.43|:80... connected.

HTTP request sent, awaiting response... 200 OK

Length: 9,765,236 (9.3M) [application/x-redhat-package-manager]


100%[=====================================================================
=======================================================>] 9,765,236
236.11K/s    ETA 00:00


22:48:01 (266.51 KB/s) - `webmin-1.250-1.noarch.rpm' saved
                   [9765236/9765236]


[root@asterisk1 webmin]# rpm -Uvh webmin*
warning: webmin-1.250-1.noarch.rpm: V3 DSA signature: NOKEY,
         key ID 11f63c51
Preparing...               ########################################## [100%]
Operating system is CentOS Linux
   1:webmin                ########################################## [100%]
Webmin install complete. You can now login to https://asterisk1.
local:10000/
```

```
as root with your root password.
[root@asterisk1 webmin]#
```

Now, we can access WebMin at the same IP address that we use to access the
FreePBX interface. So, for example, if we use port 10000, then the IP address will be
`http://192.168.243.128:10000/`.

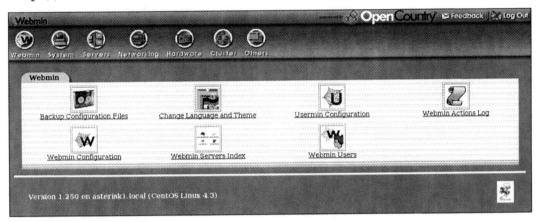

We can now log in to WebMin using our user **root** and the password we have been
using for console access in the installation chapter.

The Sky is the Limit

If we can envision an application that can be controlled via the telephone, there is
a good chance we can create it with Asterisk. Some examples of projects that are
possible with Asterisk include:

- RSS readers using text-to-speech engines
- Movie listing and screen times
- Employee time clock
- Controlling a television DVR
- Home automation using X10 controllers
- Interactive games
- Bluetooth presence detection
- Monitoring of health sensors with automatic emergency dialling
- Babysitter monitoring
- Home/Business burglar detection and alarms
- Calendar system with phone call reminders

Summary

In this chapter, we had a look at some of the more advanced options that we can use in our TrixBox system, from manually editing the configuration files to adding in custom trunks. We've also seen how to add some additional capabilities by installing tools such as WebMin. It's important to remember that our TrixBox system has CentOS at its core, so we can treat it like any CentOS server and install all the tools we like to use in managing our servers.

9
SugarCRM

CRM stands for **Customer Relationship Management**. This refers to a system that allows us to manage our contacts, leads, accounts, and sales, and helps us with forecasts and projections. SugarCRM is one of the leading open-source CRM products available. It can help many companies organize their sales flow with more features than most companies may ever want.

We may be anxious to know why SugarCRM is bundled with TrixBox. The reason is that SugarCRM is already integrated with Asterisk and, since many users are installing TrixBox systems in small to medium businesses, including SugarCRM is a great way of starting to play with it. Whenever a remote phone number is displayed, such as in contact lists or account details, a **[call]** button can be seen. Clicking on the **[call]** button will initiate a call between the on-screen phone number and our extension. This saves us from having to pick up the phone and dial the digits. This may not seem like much, but if we make a lot of phone calls, this is a real nice convenience issue.

Although going through everything we can do with SugarCRM is well beyond the scope of this book, we will take a look at how to configure the settings within SugarCRM to make it work with our phone system and a basic overview of some of the main sections of SugarCRM. For more details on SugarCRM, you can refer to the book *Implementing SugarCRM* from Packt Publishing (ISBN 1-904811-68-X).

Initial Login

When we first visit the SugarCRM application, we will see the main login screen. At this point there are no accounts set up, so we will need to log in as the administrator. For user name, we will use **admin** and for the password, **password**.

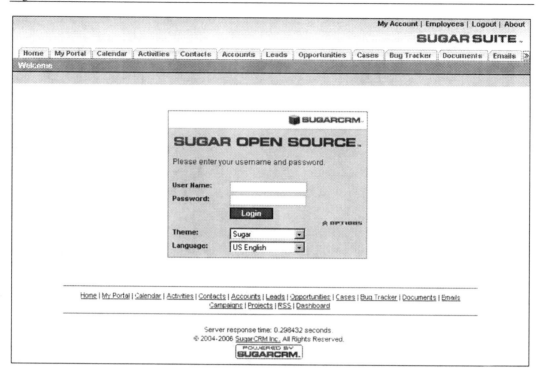

Once we are logged in, we will reach the main dashboard. This is a little overwhelming at first when we begin to use SugarCRM but it all makes sense after we spend a little amount of time working with it.

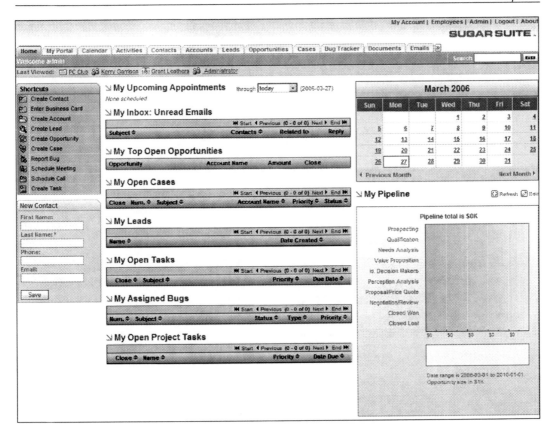

This screen is presented to all administrators and users when they first log in to SugarCRM. Here the user can manage their workflow by dealing with any emails, cases, leads, tasks, etc. assigned to them.

The **Shortcuts** section on the top-left menu allows the user to access various common areas as shown in the following screenshot:

We can create new contacts for the system by clicking on the **Create Contact** link. The following screenshot shows the basic information we can add to our contacts. There are a lot of fields that can be filled in here. These contacts will be available for us to use in other areas of the system for scheduling tasks and so on. We can also use them for one-click dialling when we configure it.

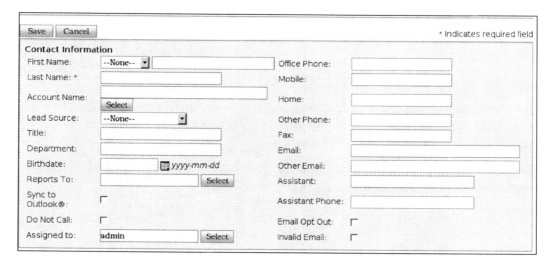

We can also enter a contact by clicking on the **Enter Business Card** link to upload a vCard. If our contact has provided us with a vCard, we can add their details by clicking on the **Create From vCard** link and browsing for the vCard file on our local file system, and then clicking **Import vCard**.

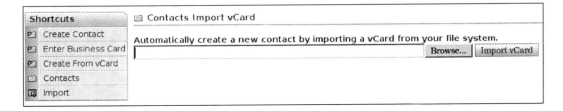

Administration

We can configure various administration options by clicking on **Admin** in the top-right menu bar of the SugarCRM interface, which will take us to the following screen:

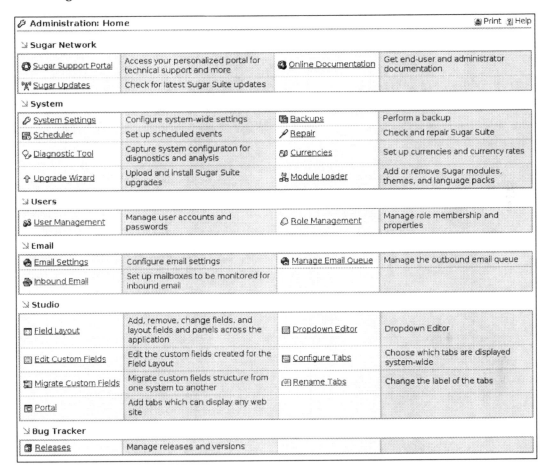

Some of the areas that are of more importance to us are:

- **Sugar Support Portal**: This takes us to a page where we can get support from SugarCRM directly.

- **Online documentation**: This takes us to the online SugarCRM documentation, which gives us detailed information on how to configure SugarCRM.

- **System Services**: This allows us to configure many internal options.

- **Backup**: This helps us to backup the SugarCRM configuration and our CRM data.

- **Upgrade Wizard**: To install updates and determine the update status.

For basic usage we can usually ignore the other areas. However, if we decide to use SugarCRM extensively, it is highly recommended that we take a close look at the online documentation and/or get a copy of the Packt title on the subject.

User Management

We should create a new user for everyone who will use SugarCRM. We can do this from the administration screen by clicking on **User Management**. In this section, we will see the following:

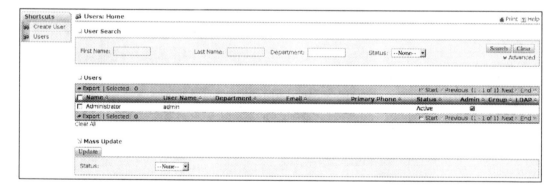

To add a new user, click **Create User** and we should see the **Create User** screen:

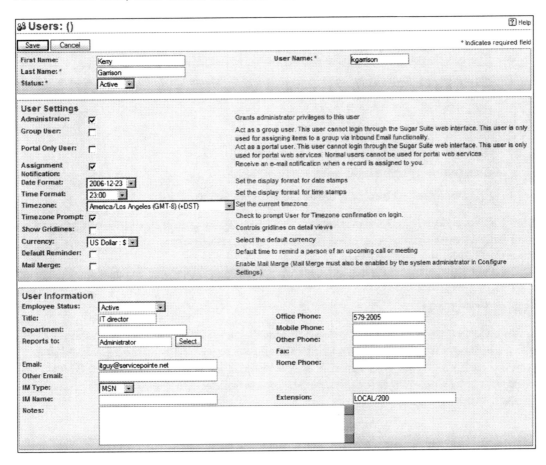

The important setting to note here is the user's extension. If this is not set properly, then the click-to-dial feature won't function appropriately. Unless we are doing something strange, the easiest way to set this up is to use the **LOCAL** prefix on the extension. This will route the call to the local extension specified. Thus, if we want to set a user up as extension 200, we would use **LOCAL/200** as the extension number.

Once we have a user set up, log in as the user and add a few accounts or contacts. When we look at a list, we will then see the **[call]** button next to the phone number.

SugarCRM has a huge number of features including the ability to manage the following types of records:

- Calendar tasks
- Activities

- Contacts (generic contact list)
- Accounts (people and companies we sell to)
- Leads (potential accounts)
- Opportunities (upcoming opportunities to make sales)
- Cases (trouble tickets)
- Bug tracker
- Documents
- Emails
- Campaigns (such as marketing campaigns)
- Projects (project tracking system with sub-tasks)

If we have a sales organization, SugarCRM can help organize our entire sales process from sales campaigns to generated leads to potential accounts, and then even tracking the entire sales process.

Summary

In this chapter, we have seen how to do some basic configuration with SugarCRM and what it can be used for within our business. SugarCRM is a huge package and as noted an entire book is devoted to the subject. If we want to use SugarCRM to manage our business it's important to become familiar with the documentation listed through this chapter.

10
Securing our TrixBox Server

You may be wondering why you need to secure a phone system. If we had built a Linux system from the ground up, we may have selected our own passwords for each component that we install. With TrixBox, every installation has the same logins and passwords and the Linux installation is not locked down from outside connections. It doesn't take much effort to do a network scan for unsecured TrixBox servers and log in using the default settings. Most installations will be installed behind firewalls; but this doesn't mean we shouldn't take basic precautions with our server. The diagram below shows a typical network layout:

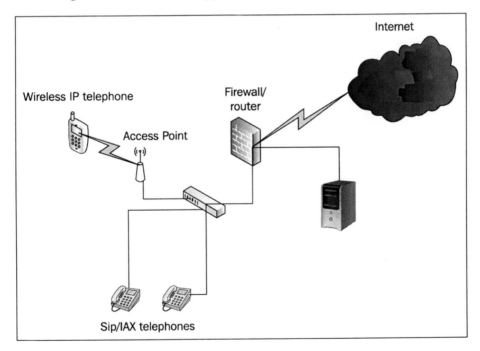

Changing Default Passwords

The main login and password for our system is the `root` account. If someone gains access to the `root` account, they have full and complete access to our entire system. This is the first thing we should change before deploying our system. Either logged in from the console or via SSH, we need to use the `passwd` command to change the root password.

```
[root@asterisk1 ~]# passwd

Changing password for user root.

New UNIX password:

Retype new UNIX password:

passwd: all authentication tokens updated successfully.
```

Secondly, we need to change the passwords for the `maint` and `wwwadmin` accounts. TrixBox includes scripts to help us with this. To change the password we use to log into FreePBX, we will use the following command:

```
passwd-maint
```

We will see the following appear:

```
-------------------------------------------

Set password for AMP web GUI and maint GUI

User: maint

-------------------------------------------

New password:

Re-type new password:

Updating password for user maint
```

The `wwwadmin` account is similar to the `maint` account except that the `maint` account allows full access to the FreePBX interface whereas the `wwwadmin` account will not allow us to see the **Config Edit** tab, where we can edit the actual config files directly.

We can change our `wwwadmin` account password by using:

```
passwd-amp
```

We will see the following appear:

```
-------------------------------------------

Set password for AMP web GUI and maint GUI

User: wwwadmin

-------------------------------------------
```

```
New password:
Re-type new password:
Updating password for user wwwadmin
```

Flash Operator Panel

The default password for the Flash Operator Panel is **passw0rd** (that's a zero not an O). If we want to change this password, there are two ways to do this. First, we can either be at the console or log in via an SSH connection and follow the following instructions:

```
cd /var/www/html/panel
nano op_server.cfg
```

We go to the line that says security code=passw0rd and replace the 'passw0rd' with the password of our choice.

```
security_code=whateverpasswordyouwant
```

Then, we do a *Ctrl+X* to exit and then a **Y** to save changes. Finally, we restart the FOP server.

```
amportal restart
```

Alternatively, we can be logged in via the web interface and click on the **Config Edit** link in the left-hand side menu. Next, we click on the /var/www/html/panel link at the top of the page and then on the op_server.cfg file on the left-hand side of the screen. On about line 41, change the security_code line to the new password we wish to use. Finally, we click on the **Update** button at the bottom of the screen and then on the **Re-Read Configs** link at the top of the screen.

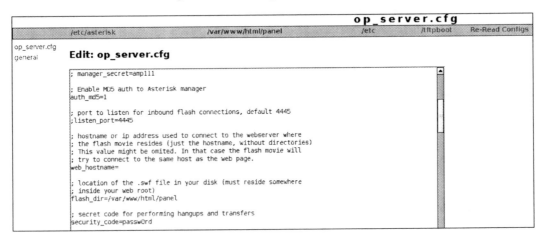

Changing the MySQL Password

The MySQL database contains all the information we need to keep our system running as well as our call-data reports. Most certainly we do not want someone else to get access to this information; so, we need to change the password before putting our system into production.

From the TrixBox main menu, we click on the **System Administration** link. Next, we click on **phpMyAdmin** in the left-hand side menu, and then on the **Database** pull-down menu in the left pane to choose **mysql**.

When we see the list of available tables, we click on the **user** table and then click **Browse**.

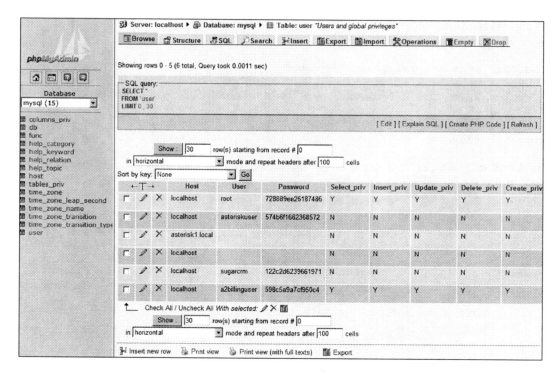

Here, we are concerned about the third entry, **asterisk1.local** for root user access. If our password field is blank, then there is currently no security at all on our database; this needs to be corrected.

Clicking on the pencil icon located beside **asterisk1.local** displays a set of records. Here, we need to click on the **Function** pull-down menu in the **password** row and choose **PASSWORD**.

We need to enter a new password, and make sure we choose one that is not going to be easy to guess. Then we click on the **Go** button to save our changes. Now if we click on the **Browse** tab, an encrypted password should be shown for both root user entries in the table.

However, this move will break **phpMyAdmin**; to fix this we need to edit the config file. We will need to be on the console or connected via SSH.

```
nano /var/www/html/maint/phpMyAdmin/config.default.php
```

The following line has to be edited:

```
$cfg['Servers'][$i]['password']        = 'passw0rd';
```

Changing the password to the one we just created, hit *Ctrl+x* and then **Y** to save our changes. Finally, we need to reboot the server and phpMyAdmin will function again.

Connecting on a Public IP Address

While we can put our Asterisk server on a public IP address, this is not recommended. If we do not have a good background in configuring Linux security and iptables, then this is a problem just waiting to happen. With a properly configured firewall, there is no reason to have Asterisk sitting outside a protected network.

Updating the Operating System and Asterisk

As discussed before, it is important to keep our system updated at the operating-system level as well as the applications. On a regular basis we should be sure to run the update script to keep our system up to date.

```
trixbox-update.sh update
```

Backups

Every system should have a good backup plan, even if it is printing all the setup screens. We will want a way to restore our configurations, should anything go wrong. Fortunately, this isn't so difficult with TrixBox; but we will need some method of dealing with the backup files once they are created.

The **Setup** link in the FreePBX main menu leads us to a **Backup and Restore** menu. Using this tool we can create a variety of backup schedules to fit our requirements. At the minimum, a weekly backup of config files and voicemail files is suggested. If voicemail is extremely important, then we can easily do a daily backup. However, we should keep in mind that a daily backup will create a new backup file every day and if we do not keep an eye on it, we could end up running out of disk space at some point.

We enter a name for our backup set and select which items we want to have backed up in the current set. Finally, we set a time to run the backup at. For a simple daily backup job, you can use the pull-down menu to select **Daily (at midnight)** as a pre-defined schedule.

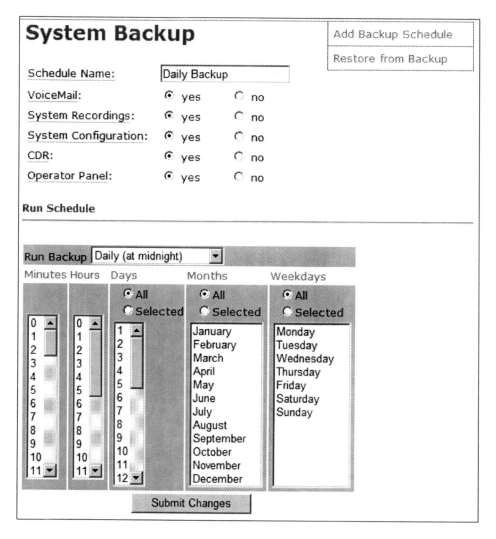

One of the easiest methods to handle remote backups is to FTP the backup file to a remote site. Assuming that you have a remote FTP site already set up, we will see how to modify the backup script to transfer the backup we set up earlier.

The actual backup is handled by a script named `ampbackup.pl` that is located in `/var/lib/asterisk/bin`. To add the lines for the remote backup, we edit the existing backup script with the following command:

nano /var/lib/asterisk/bin/ampbackup.pl

Before the last line of the file, we add the following code:

```
open(FILE, ">/tmp/ftp2remote") || die "Failed to open ftp2remote\n"
printf FILE "user username password\n";
printf FILE "binary\n";
printf FILE "cd asterisk\n";
printf FILE "lcd /var/lib/asterisk/backups/$Backup_Name/\n";
printf FILE "put $Stamp.tar.gz\n";
printf FILE "lcd /var/www/html/maint/backup/\n";
printf FILE "put asteriskathome_backup.tar.gz\n";
printf FILE "bye\n";
close(FILE);
system ("/usr/kerberos/bin/ftp -u ftpserveraddress< /tmp/ftp2remote
> /dev/null2>&1");
#system ("/bin/rm -rf /tmp/ftp2remote > /dev/null  2>&1");
```

We should make sure to change the username and password as well as the FTP server address before saving the changes with *Ctrl+x* and **Y**. Now every time our backup runs, it will FTP the files to the remote FTP server.

Additional Security

We can never be too careful when it comes to having a system online and most vulnerability comes from other services that are installed and running by default. Pasting the following code into a shell prompt will disable all the unnecessary services to help protect our system as well as provide a little performance enhancement.

```
chkconfig kudzu off
chkconfig rawdevices off
chkconfig pcmcia off
chkconfig portmap off
chkconfig rpcidmapd off
chkconfig haldaemon off
chkconfig mdmonitor off
```

```
chkconfig netfs off
chkconfig isdn off
chkconfig rpcgssd off
chkconfig iptables off
chkconfig irqbalance off
chkconfig vsftpd off
chkconfig auditd off
chkconfig smartd off
chkconfig readahead off
chkconfig microcode_ctl off
chkconfig cpuspeed off
chkconfig messagebus off
chkconfig readahead_early off
chkconfig nfslock off
chkconfig lm_sensors off
chkconfig ircd off
chkconfig autofs off
reboot
```

Summary

We should keep in mind that an Asterisk server is just a computer system and is as vulnerable to breaches and hardware problems as any other computer. Hardware problems and failures are a fact of life and caution should be taken with an Asterisk server as with any other server. With proper security measures and a solid backup strategy our Asterisk system can be well-protected and guarded against any catastrophic problem.

A

Commonly Used VoIP Terms

This Appendix covers some acronyms and terms used throughout the book, which are also common terms in Telephony. The Appendix can be used as a quick reference to the terms when reading the book or while configuring the TrixBox system.

ACD: Automatic Call Distributor is a feature used to route calls in a call center environment to the appropriate person based on factors such as availability, call usage, time, etc.

Agent: Member of a queue.

AGI: Asterisk Gateway Interface.

ATA: Analog Telephone Adapter, a device used to connect an analog phone to a digital line.

BRI: Basic Rate Interface. This is an ISDN communications standard for voice capabilities.

CDR: Call Detail Record. This is the log of a call.

Codec: A Codec is a piece of code that encodes or decodes audio using a given type of algorithm.

CRM: Customer Relationship Management.

DID: Direct Inward Dialing simply refers to the phone number dialled by a caller to reach our telephone system.

DISA: Direct Inward System Access.

Firewall: A device that exists at the border of two or more networks or network segments, and applies policies to the traffic that traverses those borders based on the security requirements of the network.

Follow-Me: This feature of TrixBox uses ring groups to allow a user to float between multiple extensions.

FXO: The Foreign eXchange Office is the end point of a connection. It is the FXO device that receives a call.

FXS: A Foreign eXchange Station is the sender of the call to an end-point device.

IAX: Inter-Asterisk eXchange protocol. The protocol is developed by Digium as a simpler and easier-to-manage alternative to using SIP for VoIP.

ISDN: Integrated Services Digital Network. This gained some popularity within small to medium-sized businesses as a cost-effective way of connecting to the PSTN and getting some advanced services, like many lines to one office or voice and data lines on one service. ISDN is a digital service and offers a few more features over POTS.

ITSP: An Internet Telephone Service Provider can deliver telephone network connectivity to our Asterisk PBX over Internet rather than over analog phone lines that need to be physically installed at our location.

IVR: Interactive Voice Response is known in the TrixBox system as the Digital Receptionist. This is the system that creates voice-prompt menus to help callers locate the appropriate person to speak to.

Hard phone: This is a hardware-based telephone.

NAT: Network Address Translation protocol.

Overhead Paging: Public Announcement System.

PBX: PBX (Private Branch eXchange) refers to the telephone switching system installed in a private location such as our office.

POTS: Plain Old Telephone Service. This is commonly used for residential purposes. POTS is an analog system and is controlled by electrical loops. It is provided by copper wires run to residences and places of business and is therefore the cheapest and easiest telephone service to roll out.

Predictive Dialer: Predictive Dialer is a software that dials ahead of a user in order to determine if the dialled number is answered by a human rather than by a fax machine or is ringing out. It is used in call centers to increase productivity.

PRI: Primary Rate Interface. This is an ISDN communications standard for voice capabilities (See also BRI).

PSTN: Public Switched Telephone Network refers to the public phone network that carries all traditional phone calls.

Queues: A call queue is a function that places callers into a waiting room while they wait for the next available agent.

Ring Groups: A ring group is a collection of extensions that will all ring at the same time when a call is transferred to the group's extension number.

SIP: Session Initiation Protocol. This is a commonly used VoIP protocol.

SoftPhone: This is a software-based telephone.

Trunk: A trunk is a channel that operates between two distinct points. This can be either between PBXs within an organization, or between the organization's PBX and its provider.

T1/E1: This is common in larger companies, although in recent years it has become more affordable. T1/E1 is a digital service and offers yet more features than ISDN, the most important feature being increased bandwidth that translates, in telephony, to more telephone lines.

VoIP: The term VoIP simply means the ability to send voice communication over existing network wires using the same methods that are used for other internet services such as email, web surfing, or instant messaging.

Index

A

ACD 147
agent 147
AGI 147
ANI 17
Applications module
  about 125
  feature codes 125
ARI 55
Asterisk
  about 14
  advantages 15
  Asterisk 1.2, features 18
  business edition 16
  digital receptionist feature 89, 91, 92
  drawbacks 15
  features 17, 18
  history 16
  name changing 21
  projects 129
  related web sites 18
Asterisk and TrixBox, difference 22, 23
Asterisk Mail Voicemail System 106
Asterisk PBX
  about 15
  standard features 103
Asterisk Recording Interface 108, 110
Asterisk server
  additional security 145
  default password, changing 140
  public IP address, connecting on 143
  securing 139
ATA 147

B

BRI 147

C

caller-id blocking, TrixBox deployment 120, 121
call queues, TrixBox deployment
  about 32
  agents 33
  planning queues 33
call queues and ring groups, difference 32
case studies, TrixBox deployment
  American Widgets Consulting Services 42, 43
  International Widgets Call Centres Ltd 43, 44
CDR 147
Codec 147
connectivity, TrixBox deployment
  about 33
  codecs with bandwidth 35
  DID lines 36
  ITSPs 35
  PSTN 33
  PSTN connectivity options, matching with cards 34
  VoIP 34, 35
CRM 147
  about 131
  SugarCRM 131
Customer Relationship Management. *See* CRM

D

DID 17, 147
Direct Inward Dialling. *See* DID
Direct Inward System Access 125
DISA 147
DISA, TrixBox deployment 125

E

Extensions, FreePBX
  about 73
  device technologies 73
  extension, editing 77, 78
  Extensions manager screen 73
  first device, configuring 75, 76
  new extension, adding 73, 74
  second extension, setting up 76
  TrixBox server, connecting to 73
  troubleshooting 76
  ZAP channel 73
extensions, TrixBox deployment
  about 28
  departmental considerations 29
  information, recording on extension num-
    bers 30
  number of employees 28, 29
  planning 30
  voicemail information 31

F

feature codes
  follow-me 126
  misc destinations 126
  paging and intercom 126
  time conditions 126
  WebMin, installing 128, 129
Firewall 147
firewall settings, TrixBox deployment 113
Flash Operator Panel
  about 56, 110
  actions performed by Flash Operator Panel
    111
  default password, changing 141
  uses 110
  using 111

free directory-assistance calls, TrixBox
    deployment 121-123
FreePBX 59
  administration page 69, 71
  Asterisk related configurations 71
  dialplan patterns 88, 89
  digital receptionist feature 89, 91, 92
  Extensions 73
  first device, configuring 75, 76
  genaral settings 99
  module administration 73
  modules 73
  modules, selecting 71
  music on-hold 98
  outbound routing 87
  queue options 95-97
  queues 94
  queues, settings 95-97
  ring group, adding 94
  ring groups 93
  ring strategy 93
  System Recordings module 90, 91
  troubleshooting 76
  trunks 79
  voice menu system 90
Free World Dialup 79
FXO 148
FXO card 25
FXS 148

G

general settings, FreePBX
  company directory 100
  dialling options 99
  fax settings 100
  international settings 101
  security settings 101
  voicemail 99

H

hard phone 148

I

IAX 148
inbound routing

about 85
configuration options 85, 86
installing, TrixBox
about 45
advanced options, accessing 46
automated installation 48-50
IP address, changing 51
media check 47, 48
time zone selection 49
Internet Telephone Service Providers.
See **ITSPs**
ISDN 5, 148
ITSPs
about 35, 148
choosing 36
IVR
about 14, 17, 148
design 40
layout for IVR system, planning 41
rules for designing IVR system 41

N

NAT considerations, TrixBox deployment
114, 115

O

open-source software
about 13
advantages 14
disadvantages 14
examples 14
outbound routing
about 87
dialplan patterns 88, 89
outbound rules 87
rule 87, 88
trunk sequence, dialplan pattern 89
outlook integration, TrixBox deployment
124
Overhead Paging 148
overhead paging, TrixBox deployment 118,
119

P

PBX

about 6, 148
backups 143, 145
custom trunk, adding 122
custom trunk, configuring 121, 122
FreePBX 69
hybrid PBX system 8, 9
traditional PBX system 7
POTS 5, 148
Predictive Dialer 148
predictive diallers, TrixBox deployment 123
PRI 148
Private Branch eXchange. *See* **PBX**
PSTN 149
about 5
interfaces 5
Public Switched Telephone Network. *See*
PSTN

Q

Queues 149

R

ring group, TrixBox deployment
about 31
configuring 31
information, recording 32
Ring Groups 149

S

SIP 149
Snap
about 124
features 124
SoftPhone 149
standard features, Asterisk PBX
about 103
active-call codes 105
Asterisk Recording Interface 108
call forwarding 103
call waiting 104
core 104
device control 105
DND 104
Do-Not-Disturb 104
Flash Operator Panel 110

info services 105
recordings 105
system-wide speed dialling 106
voicemail 106, 108
voicemail menu options 107, 108
wakeup calls 111
weather report 111, 112
SugarCRM
about 55, 131
administration 135
administration options, configuring 136
administrators and users screen 133
features 137, 138
initial login 131, 132
new contacts, creating 134
new user, creating 136, 137
records, managing 137, 138
shortcut section 134
user management 136, 137
system administration, TrixBox
about 58
Asterisk Info tool 60
Config.Edit 59
Endpoint manager tool 61
FreePBX 58
HUD manager tool 62
system configuration, TrixBox
about 52
SMTP Server setup 52, 53
updating TrixBox 52
web interface 54
system tools. *See Also* **system administration, TrixBox**
Munin 66
phpMyAdmin 62
SSH Terminal 65
System Info 63, 64
System Maint screen 64, 65

T

T1/E1 6, 149
T1/E1 cards, TrixBox deployment 117, 118
TAPI 124
telephones, TrixBox deployment
about 37
hard phones 37

soft phones 38
TrixBox
about 5, 21
add-in cards 25
additional information 50
additional security 145
advanced options, accessing 46
advantages 23
ARI 55
automated installation 48-50
backups 143, 145
components 21
configuration 69
configuration page 70
Customer Relationship Management 55
default password, changing 140
deployment 27
dialplan patterns 88, 89
digital receptionist feature 91, 92
downloading 45
Flash Operator Panel 56
future 26
hardware needed for TrixBox 24, 25
inbound routing 85
installing 24, 45-48
IP address, changing 51, 52
limitations 23
media check 47, 48
MySQL password, changing 142, 143
obtaining 45
outbound routing 87
queue options 95-97
queues 94
queues, settings 95-97
ring group, adding 94
ring groups 93
ring strategy 93
securing 139
skills required for using TrixBox 23
standard features, Asterisk PBX 103
SugarCRM 55, 131
using 24
TrixBox components
about 21
Asterisk 1.2 22
automated installation tools 22
CentOS 4.3 21

Cisco XML services 22
Digium card auto-config 22
festival speech engine 22
Flash Operator Panel 22
FreePBX 22
Sugar CRM 22
Wake-Up AGI script 22
Weather AGI script 22
TrixBox deployment
areas of concern 28
call queues 32
case studies 42
connectivity 33
extensions 28
fax requirements 42
features 113
Interactive Voice Response 39, 40
planning 27, 28
ring group 31
telephones 37
TrixBox deployment, features
advanced reporting tools 124
caller-id blocking 120, 121
DISA 125
firewall settings 113
free directory-assistance calls, making 121-123
NAT considerations 114, 115
outlook integration 124
overhead paging 118, 119
port forwarding 114
predictive diallers 123
T1/E1 cards, configuring 117, 118
Zaptel cards, configuring 116, 117
trunk 149
trunks, FreePBX
about 79
connection settings 80, 81
IAX trunk, creating 79, 80

inbound routing 85
incoming settings 81, 82
outgoing settings 80
PSTN trunk, setting up 84
route, configuring 82, 83
trunk, setting up 79-82, 84
VoIP trunk, setting up 79

V

vertical activation codes 103
Voice over Internet Protocol. *See* **VoIP**
VoIP
about 9, 10, 149
advantages 10
choosing 10
terms, commonly used 147

W

web interface
ARI 55
Customer Relationship Management 55
Flash Operator Panel 56
SugarCRM 55
system administration 58
system configuration 54
system tools 62
voicemail 55
voicemail and recordings 55
Web MeetMe Control 57

X

X-Lite SoftPhone 75, 76

Z

Zaptel cards, TrixBox deployment 116, 117

Thank you for buying
TrixBox Made Easy

Packt Open Source Project Royalties

When we sell a book written on an Open Source project, we pay a royalty directly to that project. Therefore by purchasing TrixBox Made Easy, Packt will have given some of the money received to the TrixBox project.

In the long term, we see ourselves and you—customers and readers of our books—as part of the Open Source ecosystem, providing sustainable revenue for the projects we publish on. Our aim at Packt is to establish publishing royalties as an essential part of the service and support a business model that sustains Open Source.

If you're working with an Open Source project that you would like us to publish on, and subsequently pay royalties to, please get in touch with us.

Writing for Packt

We welcome all inquiries from people who are interested in authoring. Book proposals should be sent to authors@packtpub.com. If your book idea is still at an early stage and you would like to discuss it first before writing a formal book proposal, contact us; one of our commissioning editors will get in touch with you.

We're not just looking for published authors; if you have strong technical skills but no writing experience, our experienced editors can help you develop a writing career, or simply get some additional reward for your expertise.

About Packt Publishing

Packt, pronounced 'packed', published its first book "Mastering phpMyAdmin for Effective MySQL Management" in April 2004 and subsequently continued to specialize in publishing highly focused books on specific technologies and solutions.

Our books and publications share the experiences of your fellow IT professionals in adapting and customizing today's systems, applications, and frameworks. Our solution-based books give you the knowledge and power to customize the software and technologies you're using to get the job done. Packt books are more specific and less general than the IT books you have seen in the past. Our unique business model allows us to bring you more focused information, giving you more of what you need to know, and less of what you don't.

Packt is a modern, yet unique publishing company, which focuses on producing quality, cutting-edge books for communities of developers, administrators, and newbies alike. For more information, please visit our website: www.PacktPub.com.

Implementing SugarCRM

ISBN: 1-904811-68-X   Paperback: 328 pages

A step-by-step guide to using this powerful Open
Source application in your business.

1.   Your complete guide to SugarCRM
     implementation – assess your needs, install the
     software, start using it, train users, integrate
     with existing systems

2.   Covers both the free and commercial versions
     of SugarCRM – get maximum benefit from the
     free version before paying for add ons

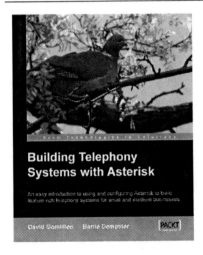

Building Telephony Systems
With Asterisk

ISBN: 1-904811-15-9   Paperback: 180 pages

An easy introduction to using and configuring
Asterisk to build feature-rich telephony systems for
small and medium businesses.

1.   Install, configure, deploy, secure, and maintain
     Asterisk

2.   Build a fully-featured telephony system and
     create a dial plan that suits your needs

3.   Learn from example configurations for different
     requirements

Please visit **www.PacktPub.com** for information on our titles

Printed in the United States
62383LVS00004B/21-52

9 781904 811930